COMPANIONS
The Strange and the Familiar

JOAN RINGELHEIM

outskirts
press

To

Ellen
who always was supportive
and taught me to do more of what made me happy.

Table of Contents

Preface   i

One: Piano   1

Two: Teaching   19

Three: The Holocaust and Women in the Holocaust   78

Four: Oral History   106

Five: Sarajevo   143

Six: Breast Cancer   165

Bibliography of Works Cited   199

Bibliography of Works by Joan Ringelheim   203

Acknowledgements   205

Preface

> How is it possible to bring order out of memory? I should
> like to begin at the beginning, patiently, like a weaver at his
> loom. I should like to say, "This is the place to start; there can
> be no other." But there are a hundred places to start.
> —Beryl Markham, *West with the Wind*

More than twenty years ago I became captivated by the title of this book. The problem was that I had few ideas about its contents. I knew that it would be a series of essays—I was not able to conceive of a book in other terms. I also knew that the title allowed a great deal of freedom in writing whatever I chose. But it took me a very long time to be able to fill the pages.

In 1997 I gave a paper, "The Strange and the Familiar," at a conference called "Humanity at the Limit: The Impact of the Holocaust Experience on Jews and Christians." As I started to think about this book, I added "Companions" to the title because it seemed to me that the strange and the familiar were always with us.

When I finally began to write, I had no intention of making the essays personal. I'm a philosopher by training, and I kept thinking solely of intellectual essays for the longest time. Then I read Mary Karr's *The Art of Memoir* and realized that the ideas about which I wanted to write were not separate from the experiences in my life and that I had to be transparent about what they meant to me. I could no longer keep the personal and intellectual separated as I had meant to do. I also realized that the issues represented by the words "strange" and "familiar" had a long history in my life, substantially predating that 1997 conference. In a 1976 paper, I wrote that "the world is both strange and precarious. Experience can often appear like a muddy river in which we grope to find our way. That groping is like trying to dissolve a portion of the strangeness so that we create some measure of familiarity ... to make the world our home."

As I look back it seems that strangeness and familiarity were themes that ran through a good deal of my thinking and feeling about oppression, prejudice, the sense of the Other as dangerous, and a range of issues that engaged me. I began to write about the parts of my life that were crucial in my struggle to meet the strange and the familiar: music and the piano, teaching, women and the Holocaust, oral history, a trip to Sarajevo after the siege, and breast cancer.

The strange and the familiar—these words and their meanings resonate in how I made sense of my life. We are born strangers into this world, with just a few instincts accompanying us at birth. As we try to become at home in our world both individually and as members of different communities, we are engaged in a constant process of chronicling, narrating, and assessing. We are trying to understand ourselves in our private and public worlds—trying to move from the strange to the familiar.

Perhaps uniquely in the liberal arts, the heart of the historian's task is "a negotiation between familiarity and strangeness," Simon Schama wrote in a 1998 *New Yorker* article, "Clio at the Multiplex." The historian attempts to bring us closer to what is distant in time, place, and culture, as well as to provide us with different understandings of what we thought was familiar. But familiarity never fully overshadows strangeness. We are in a constant negotiation between a strangeness that never quite goes away and a familiarity that never quite takes hold.

Being at home in the world must include understanding but not necessarily comfort with that world. My 1997 essay concerned the Holocaust, and while I wanted to write about the Holocaust as something with which we needed to become familiar, it was clearly not something about which we could feel comfortable in human history. Given the existence of much that is evil, it is important to remember that our struggle as human beings to negotiate between the strange and the familiar does not always bring a sense of being at home in the world.

When I finished the essays and reread them, I was struck by how often I expressed fear and insecurity about the choices I made. As a matter of fact, I almost didn't recognize myself in the anxious, self-critical person who often emerges in these pages. I suppose I could blame my mother, whose judgment I feared as a child—I wasn't good enough, I didn't practice the piano enough, I didn't care enough about clothes and boys—but she and my father were very supportive too, often praising me, being affectionate, and telling me I was wonderful. Perhaps it makes more sense now to talk of the trajectory of a life rather than speculate about parental or psychological causes.

I think that the choices I've made, no matter why I may have made them, demonstrate a wholeness to my life. It has been suggested to me that my interest in social justice had its roots in my connection to the Holocaust. I don't know if that's true, but I recall that when I was eleven or twelve, I was told that my father's parents and his youngest brother were killed by the Nazis, along with perhaps eighty more relatives who perished during Holocaust. As a young person I was quite sensitive to issues of anti-Semitism, and as a student at Oberlin Conservatory, I declined to attend the junior year abroad planned for my class in Salzburg, Austria, and subsequently decided to leave the conservatory. I suspect these decisions may have had something to do with Austria's capitulation to the Nazis and the murder of my grandparents and youngest uncle, though I don't remember thinking about this consciously.

When I was in college, I called my father to tell him that I had been dating someone who had photos of Nazis on his closet door. Whenever one of them was killed or caught, he put a cross mark through that Nazi's photo. He seemed obsessed, and this disturbed me deeply. I told my father that I wanted to come home so we could talk about it, and he spoke of his parents but said he did not want me to think about the Holocaust only in Jewish terms. He was adamant that I think about the Holocaust in terms of human beings being killed. His approach seemed different from that of many others.

It seems to me now that after this conversation I did begin to think about the Holocaust in different terms, as having commonalities with other forms of oppression, if much more horrific in scale and degree. I had already been concerned with such forms of oppression as the rounding up of the Japanese during World War II, American racism, the dropping of the atom bomb, and genocides in various parts of the world. These interests grew as I entered graduate school. During my last year I made a list of what I wanted to teach after I earned my PhD in philosophy. The list was a long one, and the only thing I remember clearly is that the first two items were anti-Semitism and racism. These were not issues that philosophers typically pursued, but I was convinced that it was crucial to try to deal with them in the classroom. They were too important to ignore. And I was desperate to make my classrooms connect with the world as it was, not just as it might be. Yet I wondered if teaching was enough. I struggled within myself about whether I should have become an activist rather than a teacher. Later, when I worked for many years at the United States Holocaust Memorial Museum, and when I went to Sarajevo not long after the siege, I struggled with the same question. I now wonder why I didn't consider teaching or my work on women and the Holocaust or my work at the Holocaust Museum a form of activism.

The essays in this book reflect these struggles. The book is finished now, but I struggle still.

ONE

Piano

For my sixtieth birthday, in 1999, I decided to buy a grand piano. The piano and its music had been an integral part of my life since I was eight years old and had become a respite from the world and my own franticness. I wanted to be able to play on a grand piano that I would cherish for the last portion of my life. It was a luxury I could finally afford.

My first thought was to get a reconditioned piano, but that proved a fruitless search. Then my friend Neenah Ellis suggested we take a trip to New York to meet Erica, a salesperson she knew at Steinway Hall. When I lived in New York City years ago, Steinway Hall intimidated me. On occasion I would walk in and quickly leave, as if escaping. The atmosphere felt imposing, and I was too nervous even to open a conversation with anyone. Was it really imposing, or was it just that I could not figure out what I wanted? Perhaps both, but when I went with Neenah, I could ignore my past experience with Steinway Hall, shed my fears and tension.

Erica and I talked about what sound I needed from the piano, what composers I played, what else I wanted. I said I played a lot of Chopin and the Romantics, that I wanted the piano to have a singing, warm sound but not as if it were under a blanket, and that it had to be capable of being brilliant and crisp at the same time. Erica escorted Neenah and me into a small room housing three pianos and a couch. "There's a piano in this room that's perfect for you," she said. "It is the only piano we have that is right for you, but don't play it if you can't afford it. Once you play it, you won't be satisfied with any other piano in the house."

I didn't ask her the price. I don't even remember wondering about it. Given what she said, I couldn't resist her sales pitch. I naïvely accepted it as if she didn't have something at stake in this process.

I walked over to one of the pianos, a Steinway B-191, and began to play a Chopin polonaise. I couldn't believe my ears, nor could I believe the ease with which my hands worked over the keys. Neenah told me later that my jaw seemed to drop to the floor. I asked Erica to play for me because you cannot hear the sound of a piano the same way when you play it as when you listen.

Erica played and I was hooked. It had a gorgeous sound. No other piano could compare with this one. Then she told me how much the piano would cost. I was floored—$53,000. It was about twice as much as I had imagined. I must have looked shocked, because Erica quickly said that I could put down a thousand dollars to reserve the piano for a month. I immediately gave her a check, even though I had to think hard about the price. I also had to do something even more practical: I had to find out whether the piano would fit into the elevator in my apartment building in Washington, DC.

After I wrote the check, Neenah and I set out to see *Wit* in an off-Broadway theater downtown. *Wit* told the story of a professor diagnosed with stage 4 ovarian cancer—a virtual death sentence. At the end of the play, after the professor died, I turned to Neenah and said, "I'm going to buy that piano as long as it fits into the elevator." Still, in spite of what seemed like a decision, I kept looking and trying out as many pianos as I could, including others at Steinway Hall, but nothing compared to the beauty of the Steinway B-191. It did fit into the elevator, just barely, and arrived in time for my birthday.

How did the piano come to be so important to me?

From the time I was five or six, I wanted to play the piano. No other instrument seemed to interest me. Pretending that the cocktail table in our living room was a piano, I would prop up a songbook and follow the notes and words while "playing" that table. And as true as this memory is, I don't know where that need or impulse to play the piano came from. Neither of my parents played the piano or any other instrument. They appreciated my playing and classical music in general, but I don't recall that the house was filled with music unless it came from me.

Once I started lessons at the age of eight, it was as if my hours at the coffee table had translated to the piano itself. Playing felt like a comfort zone to me, but even so, there were things about my attraction to the piano that troubled me, certain ambivalences or craggy edges. It took me decades to realize that these were rooted in deep feelings I had about my identity and how I wanted to be perceived, and that they played a role in my eventual decision not to pursue music as a career.

I was in high school when my piano teacher, Murray Dranoff, took me to my first live concert, at Woolsey Hall in New Haven, Connecticut, not far from my home in Bridgeport. I was sitting way back in the balcony, and I don't remember who was playing or what was played, but I do remember feeling shocked that the audience was not paying what I considered proper attention to the musician. When I now think about my decision not to play the piano professionally, I wonder how influential this concert may have been. Did I want to be in front of an audience that might be so disrespectful? Could I stand it? Did it frighten me more than I knew?

Maybe, but another incident, one that is riveted in my memory, may also have contributed to my not wanting to be a professional pianist. For reasons that weren't clear to me, my mother sent me to a new teacher, Adelaide Cohan, who had quite a reputation in Bridgeport. I think I was about twelve at the time, and although I went along with my mother's decision, I was not happy about it. Adelaide frightened me. Even my father, who loved hearing me play, would not come into her house during my lessons. He simply sat in the car and waited for me.

One evening Adelaide told me that during next week's lesson I would make a mistake in a Chopin polonaise I was learning. She didn't just say that the piece was difficult, she said that in one particular measure I would make a terrible mistake. And the following week I did just as she predicted. She proceeded to throw an exceptionally thick book of Mozart sonatas at me. She didn't hit me only because I got out of the way. When I began to cry, she sneered and asked in a more than judgmental tone, "Why are you crying?" I managed to answer, "If anyone talked to you the way you talked to me, you'd cry too." Somehow I got myself out of there.

I hid my tears from my father. I tried to hide them from my mother, but I was not able to sit at the piano—let alone play—without crying, and I finally had to tell her what had happened. She wanted me to talk with Adelaide, but I couldn't do it. It was all too much for me. It fell to my mother to tell Adelaide that I would no longer be taking lessons from her because of the thrown book. In this vein she suggested that Adelaide could get more flies with honey than with vinegar. In spite of the relief I felt about not having to continue with Adelaide, there were after-effects. While the incident was brutal, I had no idea that it would have such a lasting impact on me. I can still see the teacher, the piano, the house—the entire event comes back to me no matter that it was more than sixty years ago.

I went back to my old teacher, Murray Dranoff, until I graduated from high school. The relationship lasted long after I took lessons from him. Both Murray and his wife, Loretta, a fine pianist and teacher herself, were like family to me. I always delighted in their company. Whenever I visited my parents in Connecticut, I went to see them. It was easy to continue to see them after they moved to Florida because my parents moved there too.

During those years with the Dranoffs, I remember sitting at the piano and practicing, but I don't have any recollection of how much or how often I practiced. I must have practiced quite a lot, because I played in recitals and auditions of various kinds, but I remember practicing more as a necessity than as a joy.

In high school, I entered a concerto contest where the prize was playing with either the Bridgeport Symphony or the Connecticut Symphony, I can't remember which. For this contest, I played the first movement of the Grieg piano concerto. Murray accompanied me, playing the orchestral part. The concerto opens with what sounds like a rumble of many instruments, and then the piano enters the fray and plays chords that traverse the keyboard from a high register to a lower one. As the accompanist, Murray played this opening with a chord that mimicked the orchestral sound. When it came to my turn, rather than playing in the minor key of the concerto, I played the chords in a major key all the way down the keyboard. Murray looked over at me in shock and surprise. I wondered what I was doing, but then I slithered back to the minor key and played the concerto movement well. I won the contest and shared the win with a clarinetist. When I was offered the chance to get a record of my choice as part of my prize, I chose Judy Garland, not Rubinstein or Horowitz or Landowska or Hess or any of the other great pianists of the day. What was going on?

In high school I dated a boy named Chuck, whom I liked a great deal. He said that he was jealous of the piano, that when I played, I was more loving with the keys than I was with him. I probably should have been appalled by what he said, but I wasn't. It was true that I was much more in love with the piano than with him. For me, there was nothing to choose. Now I wonder what I was doing or feeling such that an inanimate object—which was not really inanimate to me—meant more to me than a person. I don't remember thinking about this very much; I do vividly remember Chuck's feelings of jealousy.

When I graduated from high school, the caption accompanying my photo in the yearbook was "Where there is a piano, there is Joan." That felt like an insult to me. I wanted a more nuanced view of myself. It now seems strange that I would regard the recognition of my musical talent at the keyboard as a reduction of who I was. Was I a prime example of Groucho Marx's famous statement in his autobiography, *Groucho and Me*, that he didn't want to belong to any club that would accept him as a member?

Recently, I looked at that same yearbook and saw that I was designated as one of two people in my class "most likely to succeed." How was it that I neglected this in my memory? Why didn't I focus on it, or at least on both statements? The idea I have now is problematic for me: it appears both that I could not accept a compliment because I had such a critical view of myself, and that I thought so highly of myself that some compliments were insufficient. This sort of conflicted response remained with me through all kinds of experiences.

I applied to music schools, not to liberal arts schools, primarily because my dad's doctor influenced me. He advised me to go to music school, saying that I could always get a degree in liberal arts but I couldn't always get a degree in music. Age would matter more in music. I had no idea whether he was right or not, it just sounded right to me.

I got into Oberlin Conservatory and went there not only because of my father's doctor but because I didn't think I could survive in a liberal arts institution; I feared that I would flunk out even though I was one of two valedictorians in my high school class. At the same time, I wanted to go to a music school that was closely associated with a liberal arts institution in case I didn't like music school. This concern eliminated places like the Juilliard School of Music or the Rochester School of Music, whereas Oberlin's music conservatory and liberal arts college coexisted on the same campus in the small town of Oberlin, Ohio.

Although I knew that I was talented, I was afraid to go to Oberlin Conservatory. I never talked about it very much. People didn't ask, and I didn't think I should talk unless I was asked. Perhaps I was too proud, or simply not versed in airing my fears. Still, when I received the letter of acceptance from Oberlin, I was thrilled. I knew it meant that I was considered good, and I found myself thinking about how wonderful a music program would be. Ambivalent or not, I wanted to do well, and I hoped I would. I may have been surprised that they accepted me. And now, when I say that I went to Oberlin Conservatory, I notice that people seem to be impressed.

Loretta and Murray thought I had genuine potential to be a concert pianist. I have no recollection of believing or disbelieving them or even thinking about their opinion. It's not that I thought they were lying to me or just trying to be nice. It simply wasn't something I knew how to focus on. It was a strange and surprising idea that I could not take in.

Music never interested me intellectually. Although I could lose myself inside the music I played on the piano, I suspect that I was never a true musician. Murray used to tell me, "You play by the seat of your pants." I took this to mean that I played with some kind of musical instinct, not with musical intelligence. It wasn't that my mind was uninvolved, but rather that I seemed to play with my body as much as or perhaps more than with my mind. I was never interested in studying composers, the history of music, or music theory. I never thought that if I knew more, it would help my piano playing. In truth, I never thought about it at all. I simply wasn't interested in music in any intellectual way.

I wonder now if I wanted to keep music away from the knowledge game I played with almost everything else. After all, I did end up becoming a philosopher. Did playing the piano involve my right brain, not my left brain? Music school, with its emphasis on music theory, made it seem more a left-brain thing, and I didn't want to go there. It isn't that I wasn't capable (although I admit to not being sure about this), I just didn't want to do that with music. When I say right brain, I am referring, correctly or not, to the creative and freewheeling side of myself. The left brain is said to have something to do with logic and order. I don't know if there is really such a difference between the right and left sides of the brain, but I do know that I had no intellectual interest in music any more than I had an intellectual interest in the piano. I simply wanted to play. I felt comfortable with and at the piano, and I wanted to play it, not analyze it.

I have been ambivalent about music and my playing all my life. When I was younger, I felt that I wanted time to do other things—like play baseball or football, or read a book, or take singing lessons—or that I wanted to be taken more seriously than I thought playing the piano allowed. Yet I kept on playing. There has always been something in the communication of music that is deeply important to my psyche. While on the one hand I seem to use the music for other than musical needs, I also crave expressing myself inside the music. When I play, I go to a place that I don't otherwise. I don't know whether to call it a spiritual place, but whatever it is, it is not a place where my intellect works. My mind isn't silent when I practice or play, but I am not arguing or trying to think logically or rationally, nor am I trying to convince someone of something. Music is another dimension for me, one that embraces the beauty of sound, the expression of my fingers and body, and something of my thinking.

Although I loved to be in public spaces and wanted an audience, I was an introvert and very afraid to put myself in a position of heavy competition in the larger world musicians faced. A degree of competition always played a role, but music involved something much more intense than what I considered to be everyday competition. I suspect that underneath my many explanations, I was too afraid even to face the fact that I was afraid. Consequently, music was not where I put myself forward, even when I journeyed to Oberlin Conservatory. I think music was a private affair for me and I did not want to make it public and expose it to the judgment of critics.

I had discovered early on that playing the piano was a way to get applause. I went to parties with songbooks in hand and played popular music so that people could sing along. I was so shy and afraid of the crowds at these parties that I used my playing as a way to get the attention I didn't know how to get otherwise. I was not good at small talk or at meeting new people without someone or something helping me, so my playing had two functions: to get attention and to hide. The dynamic was complicated and represented my own relationship to people who made me feel uncomfortable and strange. I used my familiarity with the music to try to bridge this discomfort.

As I thought about my future, I decided to be practical and enroll in the music education program at Oberlin. Then, a few months into my first year, two things happened. First, I heard some senior pianists play, and worried that I could never reach their level of proficiency. I never thought about the fact that I would improve by the time I was a senior. Second, my fantasies about teaching music left me parched. It was clear to me that what seemed the most practical of decisions—going into education—did not interest me for a life's work.

Furthermore, Oberlin was about to begin a semester abroad in Salzburg, Austria, for all conservatory students. My class was to inaugurate the program. As attractive as this probably was for most students,

I found myself not wanting to go. For me, it meant that I could take even fewer academic courses than the puny number previously listed in the conservatory catalogue. I now suspect that I was also afraid of this adventure and couldn't admit it because the fear may have had something to do with the fact that my family had lost scores of relatives in the Holocaust.

During my first semester at Oberlin, my music theory class was almost my downfall. My comedic instincts seemed to be my only barrier to failing that course. I used my funny side to win the teacher over, and for some reason he didn't flunk me. I felt incompetent. I could never get my head around the complexities of music theory, and apparently I didn't want to. I did better in music history, but I don't remember liking it much, whereas I loved my classes in political theory and religion. I craved sitting in the library and reading because I felt more at home in the conceptual world. I simply didn't know how to talk about music, nor did it seem as if I wanted to learn how. Words were not what linked me to music. Words linked me to other subjects, as is still true today. I now think that I never really wanted to do more than play the piano for myself.

After a few months at Oberlin, I went to my piano teacher, Mr. Koberstein, to ask if I could change my major from music education to piano. Did he think I had the talent to become a concert pianist? I wonder now where this question came from. Could I have seriously been thinking about a concert career? Apparently so, though I don't remember that. Perhaps I was ready to be influenced if someone I respected thought it was a possibility, since I didn't have any ideas about another occupation.

Mr. Koberstein said something that transformed the direction of my life: "If Myra Hess walked in the door and asked me the same question, I would tell her no." I was taken aback—Myra Hess was a world-renowned pianist—and when I asked why, he said, "It doesn't matter how much talent you possess. There's no guarantee that you could have a career, especially in the United States with so few booking agencies."

I talked with no one else. I walked around the Oberlin campus trying to figure out what to do. For some reason, I didn't fantasize a future filled with failure but with success. What if I became the female equivalent of Arthur Rubinstein? Would I want that life? I didn't think about Myra Hess or any other female artist. My own sexism must have been rampant in these private conversations with myself. (To be fair, the times were such that most of us didn't think about female achievement in the same way we thought about male achievement.) I fantasized Arthur, the male person who was one of the greatest and most famous of all pianists, and somehow this fantasy brought me to what I thought was a reasonable conclusion: this was not the life I wanted to live—too much traveling, too many audiences. It didn't feel rooted enough for me. I liked being on the stage, but confronting the stage with a piano on it was too much for me. It was a fearsome activity. I also thought there would be something much lonelier in this existence than I wanted. I didn't think I could survive in the world of musicians. Learning piano music and playing the piano didn't matter to me the way it seemed to matter to real musicians.

Looking back, I suspect I knew that my fantasy of success as a famous pianist could never be lived out and would end in failure. My current piano teacher, Betty Bullock, recently asked me whether I ever thought about becoming a non-famous musician. What a question! It's interesting that this thought never occurred to me. I didn't want a career as a musician, but I never considered the different ways of being a musician. I was not terribly imaginative, at least on this score.

Once I decided that neither music education nor a career as a concert pianist was for me, I had to leave Oberlin Conservatory. The decision has always felt right, but I now think that it would have made sense to talk more before making such a final decision. I talked with no one after that original conversation with Mr. Koberstein. I probably didn't want to have other alternatives thrown at me. I wanted to make this decision, and I didn't want further conversation to dissuade me.

For the second semester of my freshman year, I left the conservatory and entered the College of Liberal Arts. After a few months, I decided to leave Oberlin altogether. At the time I told friends that I was not sure I could live with the idealism that seemed rife on campus or that I trusted it. The place seemed too unrealistic, and I didn't believe that I would learn to live in the real world if I remained. I also suspect that I thought I would not succeed there. Once again, I must have been really afraid without realizing it. Further, and perhaps even more important, I had never been away from home and was profoundly lonely in spite of my new friends.

I applied to other schools. My recollection is that Barnard and Radcliffe, both highly competitive, said that my music credits would not translate into credits for a liberal arts degree and hence they could not admit me. However, I have no copies of letters from either place, and I now wonder what they actually said. I also applied to Boston University and was accepted. Even though I had declared in high school that I would never go there, I had no other choice: I'd only applied to those three schools. I'd been frightened to go to Oberlin, and now I was frightened to go to BU because it did not seem to be in the same league as Oberlin, which had such a good reputation.

In spite of my decision that I did not want to be a musician, I also felt guilty about going to BU because I would not be in pursuit of a career in music. Leaving music school was a sign that I did not respect my talent. Consequently, I did not play a piano for many months. I had no idea what I wanted to do or what to major in. I was confused. Still, I felt some relief that I was no longer attending a music school.

When I arrived at BU in 1958, I was housed in an apartment building converted for transfer students, except for one apartment. One day as a few newly minted friends and I were walking down Commonwealth Avenue, we passed some bureaucratic-looking buildings that included the music school. My companions asked if I would play for them. I agreed although I had no idea whether I could play anything at all. We walked the halls until we finally found a free practice room. I sat down at an upright piano and played the first few lines of a Chopin etude (Opus 25, No. 1) commonly referred to as the Aeolian Harp Etude. I went on to the first few lines of a Chopin prelude (Opus 28, No. 15) often known as the "Raindrop" Prelude. When I couldn't finish either piece from memory, I put my head down and cried. I was both embarrassed and deeply sad. I think I felt as if I had betrayed myself.

After we returned to our dorm, one of my friends, Joan Goldsmith, talked with the woman on the first floor who had held on to the one non-student apartment in our building. Joan knew she had a piano and asked if I could play it. Surprisingly, the woman agreed. After that I played piano a few times a week. Often the woman left her door open so the students who lived in the dorm could sit on the steps going down to her apartment and listen to me play. This time was very special for me. I had an audience who appreciated me and what I played. And I could finally play without being graded on the outcome.

I would not have been able to ask that woman if I could play her piano, and I doubt I would ever have gone back to music without the support of my friends. Because Joan succeeded in getting permission for me to play, I soon got over my guilt about not making music my profession. I knew that playing the piano could still be an important part of my life even if it would not be my profession. It was then that I could begin to go over a lot of music I had worked on before and during Oberlin.

In those BU years and throughout my life, I might stop playing for a week or even months at a time, but I never really stopped playing. Sometimes I would even try out a teacher just to see what would happen, but none of them clicked. I did not aggressively look for a teacher, though, even many years later when I lived quite close to the Levine School of Music in Washington, DC. I didn't take lessons regularly until 2005—a long distance from 1957 at Oberlin.

It was in 2005 that I met Betty Bullock, who has been my teacher ever since. I called her because my piano tuner suggested she might be available. What a coincidence that she had graduated from Oberlin Conservatory and even become a dean there. On the phone, I liked her immediately. She said that if we didn't click she would help me find someone else. Almost as soon as I walked into her studio, I thought we could work together. After one lesson, I knew we could. Not only was she direct, she was able to get me to work through a piece as if through the layers of an onion. She would peel music slowly so that I was not overwhelmed by its complexity all at once. In time the complexity of a piece would be revealed, and I or any student would be ready for it.

Long before I found Betty, I was often trying to figure out my relationship to music and the piano. The confusion never really stopped. It was the same with the profession I finally chose. In the middle of my graduate work in philosophy, I decided I should get out of the field. I wondered what philosophy was for. Was I doing anything constructive? I would spend six hours on a logic problem or a few paragraphs of Kant or Hegel. Did I know anything? Could I come to any creative or insightful conclusion? Could I teach? The questions came faster than any answers. It was all so reminiscent of what happened to me at Oberlin Conservatory.

Given these questions, I decided—without benefit of a piano teacher—to audition for a Tanglewood summer scholarship. I had not been practicing for months. For some reason I chose to play Gershwin's *Rhapsody in Blue*, not a piece designed to ingratiate me with Tanglewood, the world of classical music, not the world of pops concerts. I suppose my choice could have been interpreted as passive-aggressive, but it was simply the only piece I could play well. At the audition, no one exhibited disgust, but when I finished *Rhapsody in Blue,* I was given a handwritten manuscript of piano music that I could not decipher, let alone play. I might as well have been asked to play the French horn. It came as no surprise that I did not win the scholarship.

I continued to study philosophy and got my PhD in 1968, though my concerns about philosophy did not abate. When I talked with one of my professors about the malaise typical of graduate student life, he suggested that I read Boethius's *The Consolation of Philosophy* and Whitehead's *The Function of Reason.* No sooner had I begun reading these books than I had a dream that has remained a warning to me about the nature and limits of philosophy and the hopes of a philosopher.

The dream takes place during the evening. The scene is one of dark, dull streets, empty except for a couple of soldiers. There is a battle that needs soldiers, and since there are so few of them, civilians are asked to go. A number of us try to convince the civilians to go. I notice a young woman reading *The Function of Reason.* When I speak with her, she refuses to put the book down. "Don't expect to live your life through reading books," I yell at her. "The only reason Whitehead could write that book was that he had lived and was living a life." When I woke up, I realized that the dream represented at least one issue that was important to me. What did it mean to live, really live, and in what respect was philosophy part of that life, and how could that experience of living be placed within the walls of the classroom? I was interested, even desperate, to find a way that the classroom could be a meaningful place beyond the intellectual process.

After a little teaching experience, I decided that studying philosophy was important because there *was* a classroom. It seemed I wasn't fascinated by philosophy itself; I was fascinated by what it transmitted, and I wasn't happy if I discovered this alone, outside the classroom.

It also seemed there was a relationship between my music and philosophy. Without communication, the playing of music wasn't enough. If a career was to be made, either in music or philosophy, an audience was essential, but the anonymity and changeability of music audiences was disturbing to me. I wanted to be able to look at and talk with the audience. When I was younger, being a musician seemed like a one-way mirror into my best practicing. It was a much lonelier existence than I felt prepared for. At the age of eighteen I didn't realize the extent to which a certain kind of loneliness would be true for all relationships to work, so I thought that teaching philosophy would enable me to overcome this loneliness

The piano and my playing continually intervened in my life.

During my first year of teaching, at DePauw University in Greencastle, Indiana, in 1968, I invited two students of mine, Martha and Karen, to my apartment for dinner. When I thought they were on their way, I sat down at my piano. I wanted them to hear me playing, I wanted to show another side of me. When they came in, Martha said she wasn't surprised that I played well, and Karen said that she was. I didn't have the courage to tell them that I'd played for them on the sly, as if I just happened to be at the piano as they were walking over. I could not be open about how much playing the piano meant to me.

A few years later, in 1971, I was teaching philosophy at Connecticut College when I was asked to participate in a show some friends were putting on. I agreed and decided to play *Rhapsody in Blue,* a piece that was obviously a constant for me. I knew it would work, and I played it the evening of the show without being nervous, which was a revelation to me, but nothing came of it. I continued to be somewhat hidden musically, except for playing show tunes at parties. People may have known that I played classical music, but I rarely played for friends, let alone strangers.

In 1993 I was diagnosed with breast cancer. At the time I had an Abyssinian cat called Foxy, an older fellow who was sick with amyloidosis. He got worse when I was diagnosed. I worried that the tension around my breast cancer made him decline, because the apartment was in a chaotic state. One day I decided to play the piano. Foxy ventured out of the dining room for the first time since becoming sick himself. He came into the room where I was playing and jumped onto the piano bench, and I thought he wanted to be close to my playing. This was such a sweet and special moment. He gave me a gift whether he knew it or not, and the telling of this story makes me wonder again and again why I kept so much of my music to myself.

From 1989 to 2007, I worked at US Holocaust Memorial Museum. In 2000, the museum held a memorial service for its founding director, Shaike Weinberg. I was asked to speak at the memorial as well as play. I decided on a Chopin polonaise and Schumann's Träumerei. This would be the first time my colleagues at the museum heard me play, and the first time I'd played in public for two decades or more. I practiced as I hadn't practiced in years. I began to hear notes I seemed never to have heard, phrases I hadn't understood before. It felt as if the music had layers I'd never noticed, each note with a meaning and structure in relation to the other notes. It was strange to find a piece anew in spite of having played it for years, an experience I would have again when I started taking lessons from Betty Bullock.

And what of playing in public? The rehearsal in the theater was fine, and I thought my nerves wouldn't get the better of me, but I was wrong. Parts of my hands and fingers were cold, parts sweaty, wet here and dry there. My hands were not as free as they'd been when I practiced. I felt partially frozen. I couldn't get my body to be really quiet so I could just feel the music and not the audience. Before playing the second piece, I must have sat there for more than a minute trying to calm myself. It felt like an eternity, and I wondered if I would ever allow myself to lift my hands and start. Finally I did, and it was okay—not what I wanted, but okay. When it came time for me to speak in front of the same audience, I found that much easier. I was really glad that I played as well as I did, but it appears that an audience, no matter how big or small, puts the focus on the performance and makes me unable to play very well or easily. I remember one musicale years ago when I was in great pain from tendinitis and not sure if I could play at all. When I finally did, the audience didn't matter because I was so focused on the piece and whether my hands would work. It was one of the best performances I ever gave because the music counted more than the audience.

Only recently have I realized how much playing piano has always mattered to me and to those who know me. When I practice I don't feel frantic—the kind of frantic I often feel about writing or even reading. The piano relieves me in ways I don't understand. I am not sure how true this was when I was young, but now my practicing is a kind of spiritual wandering. Playing piano is part of what I do. There is something natural for me at the keyboard. It feels as if that is my place. Where do I go when I play? I don't know, except that it is a clear place where I am consumed by something beautiful.

Someone once asked me whether I practiced or played for fun. I answered that practicing was pleasurable for me but serious. I think it is different simply to play for fun than to practice for some deeper purpose. Playing piano for me is both deeply enjoyable and deeply serious, much more than a matter of "fun."

It's possible that I had the talent to become a professional musician, but I'll never know. For years, I didn't think it was even possible for me to become a musician, even a non-famous one. I chose to become a professor of philosophy because I needed an audience and I needed to feel that I was doing something to help someone—in this case, students. If filling people with music did not feel like enough for me, I hoped filling them with a passion for critical thinking would.

TWO

Teaching

It was the last day of the semester. Students were swarming out of our philosophy classroom: the talkative ones, the quiet ones, the inattentive ones—all the students I had hoped to entertain, if not to hold their intellectual interest. One of them stuck around to ask me why I became a teacher. "Because I did not go on the stage," I said. She laughed because she thought I was joking. I laughed too, nervously, because I was surprised at my apparent openness in admitting that teaching was a performance for me, and in its own way a substitute for being on the stage.

Performing on the piano could not provide the back-and-forth of ideas that a classroom offered. After high school, when I went to Oberlin as a student in the music conservatory, I longed for the intellectual stimulation I got from the political theory and religion classes I was allowed to take at the school's liberal arts college. I would race to the library after I practiced piano so I could engage with the intellectual challenges presented by those classes.

But that doesn't entirely account for my choice to teach, much less to teach philosophy. In 1962, when I was a senior at Boston University, one of my favorite professors, Dean Hosken, who taught in the Department of Religion, asked me what I was going to do after graduation. When I said I didn't know, she said, "What about teaching?" When I firmly said no, explaining that I had no interest in teaching in grammar school or high school, she was surprised. She said she meant teaching in college.

I was completely taken aback. No one had ever suggested this to me, and I'd never once thought about it as a choice. My mother had only been able to complete the eighth grade, and my father had finished high school and taken one or two college courses at night. I couldn't recall anyone in my family going to graduate school, nor did I know many women who went to graduate school, let alone to earn a PhD. I did not identify with feminism in any way at the time, but I was intrigued and complimented by Professor Hosken's suggestion, which prompted me to think seriously about getting my PhD and teaching at the college level. I even became enthusiastic about the possibility, perhaps because it was the only idea I had. I don't remember thinking about the connection between teaching and the stage at this point.

At Boston University in the 1960s, Introduction to Philosophy was a required course for everyone who graduated from the School of Liberal Arts. It was fortunate that I transferred from Oberlin to BU, because I never would have taken a philosophy course on my own. I thought then that philosophy was for geniuses or crazy people, and I didn't think I was either, yet when I took the class, I was completely engaged with the issues raised in discussion and in our reading. When I had to decide what I might teach, I chose philosophy. I remember telling myself that if I taught philosophy, I could speak about issues that mattered to me. It didn't seem that other fields opened up so many possibilities. In addition, I found to my surprise that I *wanted* to study philosophy.

When I went home to inform my parents that I was going to grad school at BU to get a PhD in philosophy, my mother said some upsetting things. First, she said that she and my father couldn't afford to send me to graduate school. I said I wasn't asking them for money because I was getting a scholarship. Then she said I would never get married, to which I replied, "If men aren't attracted to me because I've got a PhD in philosophy, the hell with them." Finally, she said that I wouldn't talk to her and my father anymore. I told her that wasn't true, that more education would not make me any more distant from them than my going to college had.

Many years later, she apologized. I accepted her apology, but I couldn't forget that original conversation. It has always haunted me. Now I think she was so afraid of what I was doing, perhaps even jealous, that she was grasping for anything that might make me rethink my decision. Although she told me that my father agreed with her, I never did ask him. Perhaps I was afraid of what the answer would be, or more likely, I simply believed her.

By the time I was a teaching fellow in graduate school, I did start thinking about the connection between the stage and teaching, and it became clear to me that there were significant differences. For one thing, teaching is a continual rehearsal with no genuine performance, whereas rehearsals for a concert or a play prepare you for a performance. For another, classrooms of students do not change from day to day, while stage audiences are different at every performance; students in a classroom participate in an ongoing process rather than the one-time encounter of a theater performance. An audience observes and responds either negatively or positively, quietly or noisily, while students are supposed to participate actively in the drama of ideas by offering ideas of their own; they are more than observers. Students are graded; audiences are not. Students are not really an audience, though when they're passive because the teacher is lecturing, they often think they are. Teachers are not soloists, though when they're lecturing, they often think they are. If, as a teacher, I make a mistake or have no time to talk about something, I can correct myself or elaborate during the next class; mistakes or omissions in a stage performance have to be handled immediately. There is no second chance for an actor during a stage performance, whereas there are many second chances for students and teachers in a classroom. The classroom is a delicate balance between student and teacher. In the best of classes, students and teachers learn from one another. The classroom belongs to both teacher and student. It is ours.

A former student, Joy, told me that I once said, "Students are who you care for them as." If that's true, it suggests that I thought a classroom could be designed and even controlled by the teacher, who could create a structure in which students played a role significantly larger than the role of an audience in the theater, or alternatively, a structure that diminished the role of students.

The teacher is something like a playwright for the classroom. When you walk into the classroom—whether you're smiling, serious, open, formal, frightened, self-confident, mixed up, or clear—you set the tone for the students. You are the only one in the room who cannot be passive because your activity provides the possibility for student activity to occur. No matter where you are, whether at a lectern or sitting in a circle with the students, your position as teacher is always center stage.

It isn't true that I went into teaching because I decided not to go on the stage. I decided that the classroom *was* my stage. In the classroom I cultivated a persona that was real but at the same time was a stage presence for intellectual work. The classroom suited me. It seemed less competitive and less difficult and lonely than life as a performer.

As a BU teaching fellow, I taught two sections of Introduction to Philosophy. I remember being very nervous before I entered the classroom, the kind of nerves you get before a performance. I never felt sufficiently prepared for a class. I would reread books I'd read ten times before so I wouldn't have to rely solely on my notes. I peppered myself with questions. Would the students understand? Was I being clear? Trivial? Complex? Not complex enough? Would I lose them if I turned my back to write on the board? Would they throw things at me? What if one of the students asked me a question and I didn't see how it applied? Well, I'd probably know the answer to the next question, but should the class be merely a kind of twenty questions? How did I keep the questions ordered? Oh my, how would I get through the hour?

One recurring dream before the teaching year began: I walk into an L-shaped room, and as I go to the top of the L, the students march out of the bottom before I say a word. Yet in spite of these dreams something substantial happened in class once I started teaching. The students were responsive, and I tried to offer them something that was not strictly philosophy so they could relate philosophical issues to their lives, a technique I would continue to use throughout my teaching life.

Difficulties arose quite early in my days as a teaching fellow. For example, exams and grading. I did not suspect how hard it was to construct a decent exam question. What constituted a good question? How could I be sure the questions were clear? Was I covering too much? Too little? Where could I find the answers to these questions? And then, after an exam was taken or a paper turned in, grading came into play with another question: how to evaluate a student's work. It had never occurred to me that it would be so difficult, even harrowing, to grade my students.

Once, I mentioned in class that I would welcome the students' responses to the comments I wrote on their papers and exams. Someone thought I was making a wisecrack and asked whether I had taken a course in the evaluation of papers and exams. The students seemed to take it for granted that PhDs were trained in various aspects of teaching. I disabused them of this view, saying that all we had was on-the-job training.

My father once watched me grading papers when I was a teaching fellow. He wondered whether I could survive without committing myself or having a heart attack. He simply saw too much nervousness. How could I teach if grading affected me so strongly? I always used a pencil so I could erase if I wanted to change what I had said, but to be honest, I never erased much at all.

I decided that I would seek applause during the last day of my first classes. I recapitulated our months of work, trying to put all the pieces together, and then I thanked my students for a wonderful semester. Though I was prompting their applause, genuine feelings were exhibited. Whatever staging I had manufactured, it worked on me and the students. Still, I knew it was showmanship. I doubt that I understood how much power and control I craved in spite of my wish to equalize the distance between student and teacher.

Although I was feeling more or less positive about teaching by then, the reality of teaching philosophy to undergraduates at Boston University didn't convince me that I was doing something important or even meaningful. I had another dream, one that made me question my whole enterprise (and one that I described in the previous essay, but I do so again). In the dream, it is evening in a town, its streets empty except for some soldiers. A battle is going on, and since there are too few soldiers, civilians are being asked to go. Many refuse. A number of people, including me, try to change their minds. (Perhaps this was a reflection of the position of the teacher.) I notice a girl reading Whitehead's *The Function of Reason*. When she refuses to put the book down, I yell at her. "Don't imagine that Whitehead was able to write that book through reading!" I say. "The only reason that Whitehead could write the book was that he had lived and was living a life." I have no idea whether what I said in the dream was true since I had no knowledge of Whitehead's life. I now suspect that the dream, being mine and no one else's, was part of a self-critique exhibiting the anxiety I had as a philosophy student, a teacher, and a human being, a fear that I would live through theories alone and not through experience as well.

The dream made me wonder about pursuing a degree in philosophy, and my worries brought me back to music. I decided to apply to a summer program at Tanglewood, got an audition, and chose to play *Rhapsody in Blue*. I played it well, then was handed an indecipherable piece of contemporary music and botched it. I did not get into the summer program, and I returned to the Philosophy Department in the fall. I felt I had no choice, and I hoped that teaching itself would overcome my doubts.

When I think back on those years, I find it hard to believe how much was going on behind the scenes of intellectual work. It wasn't just that a lot of students were sleeping with professors, it was also that sexuality in some form played a role in so much of what happened on campus. As an undergraduate, I had a professor of political theory, Murray Levin, who announced to me that women always wanted him to leave his shoes under their beds and didn't I feel the same? I told him no, not in the least. A professor in graduate school, Milic Capek, said that I didn't take courses with him because I found other professors more physically attractive. Still another reported that when I told him that a professor who had groped a student was interacting with children (by which I meant students who were considerably younger and often naïve, like me), he decided not to have an affair with me. However much the feminist movement mattered to women, the sexual revolution seemed to matter more to everyone. For a time I worked as secretary to a married professor of philosophy and physics, Robert S. Cohen, and I did have an affair with him, but I let myself believe that nothing was really going on because I could not fully reckon with the situation. It was too much to handle.

Often a situation became untenable. One day I went to talk to Professor Henry Ruf about a philosophy of language paper. We had never spoken about anything that did not have to do with philosophy. I had never thought of him in any sexual way, nor had he expressed any interest in me, but all of a sudden, as we started to speak about my paper, he rose from his desk, grabbed my arms, and dragged me into the coat closet, a long narrow space with clothes hooks on the wall. I was stunned. He didn't kiss or fondle me, he just kept dragging me deeper into the closet. I struggled and eventually was able to free myself from his grip. I ran out and went to my friend Donald Dunbar, who was also getting his PhD in philosophy. When I told him what had happened, he charged to Henry's office, climbed up on the desk brandishing an umbrella, and said, "Leave her alone, she's mine." It was a long time before I fully took in what had happened that day with Henry and what Donald had said. *She's mine?*

Forty or so years later, I ran into Henry at a conference and asked him what he'd been thinking when he dragged me into that closet. He played ignorant, claiming he had no idea what I was talking about, but then he admitted to the incident. When I asked him again what he thought he was doing, he said he assumed I would comply. I asked no more questions. I think I was stunned. I remember leaving, but I have no recollection as to whether I said anything, though I would like to believe I offered some retort. Needless to say, he never apologized.

Various gender issues were as rampant as sexuality, and of course the two were always connected. One example: I was going to be the first woman in years to receive the Borden Parker Bowne Fellowship from Boston University's Department of Philosophy. At the time it was the only award for graduate students in philosophy. The department chair, John Lavely, called me into his office and asked me to give up the award in favor of a male student who had a family. He said this student needed the money more than I did because I was single. Donald Dunbar had warned me that this might happen. I don't know what I might have said without that warning, but when confronted with a choice, I refused to give up the fellowship. No woman had been awarded this honor in more than fifty years, and I was not about to throw it away.

Although I was very good at teaching undergraduates at BU, landing a full-time job after I received my PhD was another matter. It was clear at the time how difficult it was going to be as a woman looking for a job, both in silly and serious ways. For instance, Tulane University was going to invite me for an interview but called to say it was impossible to do so. Why? Because there were no women's bathrooms on the floor where the department resided, they told me.

During an interview at American University, I met with the chair of the department. He quickly announced that he didn't know if he could hire a woman since women get married. Taken aback, I said something on the order of, "Well, you could introduce me to someone in the area, and then I might not leave." My response was rather weak and odd given what he had said. I did ask whether he had ever had such an experience when he hired a woman. He said, "No, a man married and left the area." His response was even weaker and odder than mine, and I left it hanging.

We made our way to the office of the dean, who repeated what the chair had said. I got angry and suggested that they both seemed to have problems with women and they should discuss this between themselves. I then opted out of the conversation, wondering why they were even bothering to interview me. I spent the rest of the afternoon with various groups in the department and seemed to impress them. At the end of the day, when I returned to the chair's office, he said, "I think we could hire a woman, but I'm not sure we could give a woman tenure." I couldn't believe my ears and simply rolled my eyes. What could I say? I must have been trying not to express my anger verbally, but now I wonder why I was so restrained. Was it just the times? When I recounted this story to my professors at Boston University, they wanted to sue. I told them not to bother, because even if we won, I didn't want to be at such a place.

I was also interviewed at the New School in New York. I flubbed the interview with the undergraduate group because I postulated that Socrates had some obligations to his wife and children and not only to his principles. They ridiculed this idea, saying that I was being a Jewish mother. In the afternoon I participated in a graduate seminar led Professor Benjamin Nelson and did quite well, but the graduate division was not offering a full-time job, and the undergraduate division said they didn't want to hire me because I refused to teach a course in aesthetics without any reading. Without any reading? Why would they make such a stipulation? I would have been happy to teach aesthetics, but I couldn't imagine teaching it or any other course without any reading. Nevertheless, that was their demand and their stated reason for not hiring me, though I suspect it wasn't the real reason.

After the graduate seminar, I went out for coffee with one of my dissertation readers, Marx Wartofsky, and Professor Nelson, who praised my participation in his seminar. As an apparent corollary to his compliment, Professor Wartofsky said that if I were not a friend of the family, he would have an affair with me. I think I smiled and took his comment as a compliment. I wasn't exactly a feminist at the time.

When I went to Greencastle, Indiana, for a series of interviews at DePauw University, I was pleasantly surprised given my previous experiences, but it was also a sad time because the funeral or memorial service for Martin Luther King Jr. took place while I was at DePauw. Dr. King's assassination did not seem to resonate on the campus. I was shocked and put off by what seemed to be the lack of concern, but I didn't say this to anyone I met, and now I wonder why. I could have asked people what they felt, I could have raised questions about what was happening on campus, because I really didn't know and had made my observation with little evidence. Why did I remain so passive when I was so sad and so concerned?

As to the interview process itself, the Department of Religion and Philosophy, especially its chair, Russell Compton, was open and willing to talk. They threw a party for me with the department members (all men) as well as their wives or significant others. I talked with professors of ethics, religion, philosophy of language, and philosophy of science. When asked what I would like to teach, I told them I was thinking about a course on racism and anti-Semitism as well as philosophy of history and history of philosophy. No one flinched. They seemed more than receptive to the idea. Unbeknownst to me, the women who came were sure that I would pay no attention to them. They assumed I would only talk with the men in the department, but they were wrong. I very much wanted to know what it was like for women on that campus.

By contrast, my interviews with members of the DePauw administration were strange. I had been warned by the members of the department that this would be the case. I met with President William Kerstetter, Dean Robert Farber, and perhaps a few others whom I don't recall. When President Kerstetter asked me about my views on protest, I delivered a long disquisition on protest in hopes that he would not fully understand my position. I now have no idea what I said, but it appeared to work, because he didn't press me further.

The dean asked whether I would object in a public way to church attendance on Sunday, a question I found very odd, but I said no. I added, with tongue in cheek, that I thought one of the benefits of being Jewish was that you did not have to get up for church on Sunday morning. He didn't find that remark funny, and proceeded to announce that some of his best friends were Jewish. Again I was shocked but said nothing. The chair of BU's Philosophy Department later told me that President

Kerstetter called and asked him whether I believed in God. I have no idea what he said, but I somehow got through the interviews with the administration.

Sometime during my days at DePauw, I was introduced to Norman Levine, a history professor, because he was Jewish. He was the only faculty member who admitted to being Jewish—others seemed to be hiding as Unitarians. All of this made me wonder about the school.

The Philosophy and Religion Department wanted to hire me. Russell Compton told me that the entire department had fallen in love with me. They made an offer, and they sent me flowers on the day I was scheduled to do my dissertation defense at BU. Perhaps there was something sexist about all this, but it felt genuine, and very different from the behavior of the other departments that had interviewed me. I think that feeling so accepted warmed my heart and won me over.

Even though I was reluctant to take the job for a number of reasons, among them that DePauw was located in a small town far from a large city, I couldn't refuse. At the time, I had no other offers. I knew that the students were quite good and the department was more open than any I had encountered so far. I thought that my reluctance may have been misplaced, so I accepted the department's offer and went to DePauw in the fall of 1968, little expecting that I would leave at the end of the second semester, in May 1969.

That first year of full-time teaching was memorable. I was more involved at DePauw than I ever was before or after. Teaching was my life there. My memories of DePauw are more vivid to me than those from anywhere else I taught in my thirteen years as a philosophy professor. After DePauw, I taught at Northeastern, Connecticut College, University of Bridgeport, SUNY/Stony Brook, and Wesleyan, and I do remember those years, but no year manages to remain so much in my memory or to matter so much as the one at DePauw.

Just before my journey to DePauw, I went to a conference on racism and poverty near Boston. It was a difficult and moving experience. I found myself screaming at what appeared to be a lack of communication or even a wish to communicate. I couldn't stand what looked to me like whites hiding from Blacks and Blacks from whites. Whites seemed to be afraid to talk to Blacks, no matter what was said. Whatever a white person said, some Black person would say they were wrong. At one point, I reached my limit, and I got up screaming, "Shit, what the hell is going on? I came for a conference between us, and if you only want to throw darts at whites, then we can make cardboard effigies and you can have a good time." I think some of my reaction had to do with a recent failed love affair. What I was experiencing at the conference replicated that situation in terms of lack of communication, so my screaming was probably over the top.

While some Blacks, especially some of the younger men, hated me, other Blacks liked my big mouth, but it was the responses of the white folks that really got to me. Any number of white men and women came over to tell me that they didn't have the courage to say what I'd said although they felt the same way and were grateful. Zack, who was Black and was one of the conveners of the conference, told me that he was glad I'd spoken up, and though he didn't say so in so many words, I suspect he thought that my outburst might have broken the ice. I came to imagine myself in relation to DePauw when I got these responses. I realized that I would have to say more than usual, and more loudly, when I felt something had to be heard.

One afternoon I went out for lunch with Zack and two other white women and one white man from the conference. We were stopped by a Boston cop who wanted to make sure we felt safe. Zack was the only Black person in the car. This was quite a lesson for us all, impossible for me to forget. I was driving, and I was scared of the cop. I think I wanted to beat him up, but I simply said we were fine.

At the end of the conference Zack asked all of us to think about what we would do afterward. He said we could never change the entire world and abolish racism in one fell swoop but we could do a great deal wherever we were. He challenged us with the question "What will I do where I am?" I went to DePauw with his words imprinted in my mind and on my soul, and I carried them into the classroom with me.

The summer before driving to Greencastle in my black VW, I read a great deal for my courses. I also read as much as I could find about the history and practices of sororities and fraternities since about eighty percent of DePauw students were part of this so-called Greek system. I felt I was going to what would be a lonely place, though I suspect I tried to forget these feelings because I had a job. In addition, I had decided to be a gadfly or a nuisance at DePauw.

When I arrived in Greencastle, it felt like a kind of flat-land prison to me, yet it also seemed that there were kind and thoughtful people there, because the department provided me with lunches and dinners as I unpacked all my boxes. I was to learn more as time went on.

Before the start of classes, I decided to go to Lake Forest, near Chicago, to see my good friend Rosalyn Sherman, with whom I roomed when we were both grad students in philosophy at BU. I needed to get away, I wasn't feeling comfortable in my new place, but the 1968 Democratic Convention in Chicago with its riots was not at all a respite as Rosalyn and I watched it on TV. It seemed I had gone from my psychological prison to an armed camp. It was more than difficult to watch. I especially cannot forget the riots, the treatment of protesters, and the speech by Senator Abraham Ribicoff condemning Mayor Daley and his Gestapo tactics.

Back at DePauw, I learned that there were perhaps 16 Jewish students in a student body of 2,500. There were more Black students than Jewish students, but not by much—only 26, as I recall. As for the faculty, I already knew that there were few women, and that only Norman Levine in the history department, along with his wife, Rose, and their family, was openly Jewish. While I had no interest in being a practicing Jew, the way in which DePauw excluded Jews or treated Jews as freaks of a sort (that was how I felt with at least one couple in the department) grated on me, and I decided that I would not teach on Rosh Hashanah or Yom Kippur. I did not go to a synagogue on those days; I stayed home and felt strange and hidden. It was clear that the administration wanted a campus populated almost exclusively by white Anglo-Saxon Protestants.

A Black student who attended my Philosophy of History class later told me that the students called me "the Jewish woman philosopher from the East Coast." I asked how they knew I was Jewish and if they had any other information. Maybe they knew my measurements too? The student was a little shocked, I think, but I was bothered by what he said. It felt odd and awful at the same time.

There were meetings for new faculty, and I remember that the first one was pretty boring. I was waiting for my chance to say something, anything apparently, because I found it hard to sit there quietly. My opportunity finally came when the discussion turned to swimming hours in the pool. Someone announced hours for faculty and administration couples and their families, but no times for single people. I said I thought the categories were rather silly and asked why they were excluding single folks. Everyone laughed except for the administration people. Nothing changed. Months later I discovered that the story of what happened at that meeting had ballooned into the rumor that I had threatened to crash the noon nude male-only faculty-administration swim by jumping into the pool alone—and nude, of course.

I had begun to make a rather outlandish impression from the very first meetings I attended, and this became my refrain at DePauw. My behavior was shocking to the administration, and to some faculty and students, but others were delighted and even energized by the things I did.

For my first lecture, I was to open a course called Basic Beliefs, which I team-taught with Bob King, professor of religion, and Russell Compton, our department chair. Russell introduced me. This class, which had about eighty students, was held in an amphitheater-like room, and because of where I was sitting in the back, I walked down the middle aisle to the lectern in front. I felt a bit like a celebrity because Russell's introduction was so warm. I thought it would be nice to give a sort of acceptance speech acknowledging my celebrity status in a humorous way before I began my lecture, but that was not meant to be. However, I was confident that the judgment of my remarks would not be filtered only through the student grapevine because an important part of the Philosophy and Religion Department was in attendance. I could only hope I would be as good as they seemed to believe. I certainly was going to try. Although I hadn't slept much the night before the class, I didn't feel nervous anymore. I felt assured.

I opened with some ideas from an article by Donald Dunbar, who had been a mentor and friend of mine at Boston University. The article, "A Concept of Teaching," spoke of opening the classroom to shared responsibilities, to the concept of everyone in a class as a learner, and to the necessity of accepting ambiguity and developing its possibilities in the class. This was my way of suggesting what we wanted in this Basic Beliefs class. Some of my listeners were intrigued, others interested, some probably bored or disbelieving, and none of us knew whether these ideas would work. We had set up a steering committee that would meet each week, and anyone from the class could attend to discuss how it was going or how it might need to be rebuilt. It was quite a fantasy, but one that captured the attention of many of us.

I began my lecture proper with Edward Albee's play *Who's Afraid of Virginia Woolf?* and Leo Tolstoy's novella *The Death of Ivan Ilyich*. I said these works raised two questions: What do you want? Who is afraid of Virginia Woolf? I quoted from Woolf's *A Writer's Diary* to put my remarks in focus: "Life is ... the oddest affair; has in it the essence of reality. I used to feel this as a child—couldn't step across a puddle once, I remember, for thinking how strange—what am I?"

I proceeded to try and engage the class through some comparisons pertaining to the readings that might be significant for the students, who were primarily in their first year. I discussed the proprietary acts we undertake to pursue what is supposed to be the proper course of life—school, marriage, job. Then I spoke of the human relationships integral to these decisions and how the so called proper course may be the least likely to sustain our involvement. Within this context I spoke of love, its limits, the protections we may need to adopt, and how they can be destructive. Lastly, I spoke of death and salvation. I tried to distinguish between actual and metaphorical death and related illusions and deceptions about reality. I quoted Ivan Ilyich on his deathbed: "What if my whole life had really been wrong?" When Ivan reflected on his life, he found that it had been a deathlike existence until his son kissed him as he lay dying; perhaps this kiss was his salvation. Then I quoted from Albee's play, centered on the marriage of Martha and George. "When people can't abide things as they are, when they can't abide the present," George says, addressing Martha, "they do one of two things ... either they turn to a contemplation of the past, as I have done, or they set about to ... alter the future. And when you want to change something ... you bang! bang! bang!" Thus, I said, it all seems to come down to death and burial or life and resurrection or salvation. And with that I ended my explorations with a repetition and extension of my original questions: Who's afraid of Virginia Woolf—that is, who's afraid to search inside? What do you want? What is right? How do you know?

In the course of the lecture, I began to feel as if the class was really listening, and it gratified me to think that what was meaningful to me might be resonating with them too. As they were leaving, Bob King came up to me and said with a smile, "That was a tour de force." How nice that he was pleased and that Russell Compton also seemed pleased. I liked what I had said, I liked how I sounded, and perhaps most of all I liked the feeling of relief that the first lecture of my first full-time teaching job was over. That said, I had to repeat this lecture in the afternoon for the second section of Basic Beliefs and another eighty students. Interestingly, a number of upper-class students showed up that afternoon and also attended the following week, apparently because some word was out about me. Whatever that meant, it was clear that some students who weren't in the class wanted to know what I was saying.

In one of the early discussion groups in the Basic Beliefs course, the students reflected on the way they lived on campus and the way they lived at home. They worried that the atmosphere on campus bred more intolerance and lack of appreciation for differences than they might find on other campuses; at the same time, they worried that they might be slaves to the way of life they had experienced at home to such an extent that they wouldn't be able to take advantage of the options offered by a more diverse campus. It disturbed them that many DePauw students were so involved in fraternity and sorority games that they forgot who they were and what they wanted and needed. Some of the guys talked about dating girls for a long time without getting to know them at all. It is not often that one gets to hear young people talk so honestly and openly about their concerns, and their demeanor changed as they began to show their emotions, their facial expressions becoming more relaxed and interested. The class was supposed to end at 11:00, but only one person had left by 11:30.

When I went back to my apartment, I felt that I had some power in the classroom, but I had no one with whom to sift through my feelings and thoughts. I was lonely and I didn't like it. Still, I had many weeks of lecturing ahead of me, and I didn't want to dwell on the life I had at DePauw because I thought it would be depressing and unhelpful.

"Self-Identity and Social Consciousness" was the topic for this first week of Basic Beliefs. The second week was to take us to a particular kind of social consciousness, namely racial consciousness in America. Our teaching team had given the class an assignment to write a one-page essay on the question "Is there evidence of racism at DePauw University?" Most of the students said that they hadn't been here long enough to speak about such matters. Few talked about the fact that there was such a small number of non-whites on a campus of more than 2,500 students. Even fewer tried to explore their own racism and how it might reflect on the racism of the campus. What seemed true was that most students in the class did not have a problem with DePauw's lack of diversity. Homogeneity was what was familiar to them.

Before my second lecture I discovered that one of the readings, *The Autobiography of Malcolm X,* had not been ordered by the bookstore; consequently, the students were reading a very good book but one written by a white author, Jonathan Kozol. I wanted to jolt them with Black writers. The racism and poverty conference I mentioned earlier kept entering my thoughts and feelings. The problem of racism made me want to scream, and I was angry at what I had seen at DePauw. I was also afraid of what might be revealed in the class, no matter that I felt it had to be let loose. I walked into class with my mouth dry; my tongue seemed stuck to the roof of my mouth, and my voice cracked. I began by talking of the racism and poverty conference, repeating and emphasizing Zack's question to those of us in attendance: What will I do where I am? I suspect I was also saying that since I was at DePauw, I would stick my neck out and into their lives.

I then gave the students a taste of some Black writers. I read excerpts from Alvin Poussaint's essay in Floyd Barbour's *The Black Power Revolt,*

Stokely Carmichael and Charles Hamilton's *Black Power: The Politics of Liberation in America,* and J. Saunders Redding's *On Being Negro in America.* I focused on a story Redding told about his son Conway, who loved to accompany his mother to a co-op market because he had struck up a friendship with another young boy, Reggie. For a time, while Conway's mother was pregnant, it fell to Redding to do the shopping with his son. "The first time I took him there," Redding writes, Conway "burst through the door ahead of me, . . . then suddenly let out an Indian whoop— 'Reggie!' and got one for an answer—'Conway!' . . . They stood looking at each other for a moment, then they came together, each with an arm around the shoulder of the other, and exploded off to play outside." This went on for several weeks, until one day Conway gave his customary whoop and wasn't greeted by one in return, although Reggie appeared. Conway sensed that something was wrong.

"I can't play with you," Reggie said.

"What's the matter, are you sick?" Conway wanted to know.

"I just can't play with you any more," Reggie said.

Conway moved a fraction closer to me, clutched the handle of the food cart I was pushing. . . . Before Conway asked the next question, I knew the answer that was coming. I did not know the words of it, but I knew the feel—the iron that he would not be prepared for; the corrosive rust that it would make in his blood. . . .

"Why?"

Reggie scowled then. . . ."Because you're a nigger, that's why." . . .

Conway looked at me wonderingly, not feeling hurt, as they say a man knowing himself shot but still without pain will look with surprise.

"I'm better than you," Reggie said, "cause my father said so."

"You are not," Conway said, but I thought he shrank a little against me.

"No, son, he isn't," I said. . . .

"You are not," Conway said, and straightened. "My daddy says you aren't."

"You don't go to my school, you don't go to my church, you don't go to the movies I go to . . . and that's because you're not good enough. Yah-yah!" Reggie said. "Niggers work for us, niggers work for us, you're a nigger."

Later Conway asked his father why he couldn't go to Reggie's school and Reggie's movies. In answer, Redding told him about prejudice, but "no one has ever made the anatomy of prejudice simple enough for children." Conway listened to his father, then said, "It's all complicated up."

Seven years later, Conway's parents received a letter from his New England preparatory school: "We have been unable to reach him. . . . He seems to prefer to be alone and will not participate in those activities for which he has undoubted talents." Redding concludes, "Perhaps there is only a slight connection [to the story about Reggie], but I would be hard to convince."

When I finished reading, I asked the class, all white, "What do you think about Negroes?" I was shaking because of what I'd read to them and because I was afraid of what they might say or feel, but also because I wasn't sure I had the courage to be honest with them or myself. The first girl to speak began to cry, saying that her paper should be torn up because she had not articulated how much fear and prejudice was in her. I appreciated her honesty. Another student said that he had lived with "them," had gone to school with "them," and because of his experiences did not want to be with "them." Other students quickly ganged up on this boy, demonstrating that they were on the right side, yet the self-proclaimed bigot became one of the few honest students in the room. I interjected that this sort of attack on the bigot was an easy convenience so the attackers could avoid some real probing about where they were in their lives: What were their feelings, their needs, their ignorance? I pushed them to think about themselves in the context of DePauw and the larger world. As we left the class, all a bit exhausted, a student came up to me and said she hadn't known that Negroes had a problem in this country. I swallowed hard and said something like, "Haven't you watched any television?" I still can't believe I said this. I must have been as nervous as a youngster getting a shot in a doctor's office.

The afternoon class went differently. After my reading, I was met with silence when I asked, "What do you think about Negroes?" The silence was loud, self-conscious, and lasted for five full minutes, probably because there was a Black student in the class. The other students didn't know what to say, and I couldn't get them to speak directly at all. I talked to the class about sororities and fraternities and the admission policy on campus. The students continually tried to avoid campus issues—the place where they lived. They eventually made some comments about the world and how difficult it all was and how they felt impotent. I kept trying to push them from where they were not to where they were. I wanted them to try and be courageous at DePauw.

After class, the Black student, Gail, came up to me and thanked me for what I was doing. I asked her to explain. She said this was the first time she had been in a group of whites where the whites were made to squirm. She had always been the center of attention as the "expert" on race. Having a white teacher who did not ask her to act as the expert and instead put the white students on the spot was a new experience for her. I'm not sure my way of handling the issue was as purposeful as Gail thought. I suspect that I was afraid of Gail because she wasn't white and I didn't really know what to do, but I think I knew in some way that calling on her would have been a mistake.

As the students were leaving, I heard myself challenging some of them to go to the admissions office and ask about possible quotas, etc. When I began to examine myself, it seemed to me that I was willing to challenge myself and my students in the classroom, but I wasn't sure if I would challenge myself *outside* the classroom. I decided that if I didn't talk with the head of admissions, Louis Fontaine, I would be a coward, so I called and made an appointment with him. A short while later, Nancy from my Philosophy of History class walked into my office, followed by Bob King. I told them that I was going to see Fontaine, and with that a dam seemed to break for me. I was angry at everyone including myself: angry at students and faculty who didn't give a damn, at the bewildered students who hadn't thought about the problem and were scared, at an administration that claimed there was no problem. I was ashamed of all our talk accompanied by little action. My reaction was enormous, and this was only my third week at DePauw. What was going on? I'm sure my state was difficult for both Nancy and Bob, not to mention for me.

Nancy began to talk about herself. She said her mind felt like lemonade and she was bewildered by her own inaction. I finally said something to the effect that education ought to be an experiment, that we ought to have enough faith in our community to take chances, to do things that might even seem outlandish and see what the results were, and damn it all, to make a community in which failure was not a sin. Bob said he was threatened by my viewpoint and my trying to enact these ideas. I didn't know what to make of his comment. Although I wanted to understand, I also did not want to hear what was going on for him. Was it because I had less to lose as an untenured first-year faculty member?

A week later I went to see Louis Fontaine. The meeting was tense from the start. He immediately asked if I was there to make trouble. I said, "No, I'm only here to get some information." This was not quite honest of me, just strategic. He offered a long comment on the admissions policy at DePauw. Afterwards, I asked about the homogeneity of the campus, and he indicated that he was beating the bushes for Blacks. He opened a desk drawer to show me examples of misspellings on the applications of some Black students he'd interviewed. There was no file, only a small pile of spelling mistakes lying in the bottom drawer of his desk just waiting to be lifted out and shown. I quietly asked him whether he saved the misspellings of white students as well. He frowned but didn't respond.

Incredibly, he admitted that he'd asked a Jewish member of a fraternity to review the applications of Jewish girls. I'm not sure what he was driving at, but it seemed to me that he was essentially using this guy to see whether the girls were attractive enough. I muttered something about pimping under my breath. Perhaps he didn't hear me, but again there was no response.

When I raised the issue of homogeneity again, he asked whether I was making a judgment or accusing him of something, whereupon he became agitated. If I was, he said, I should leave. I said no, I was just describing the campus, but of course I *was* making an accusation. I was really ready to shout at him, but I was determined not to raise my voice or speak in anything but neutral tones. At that point, he ended the meeting by saying again that he hoped I wouldn't start any trouble. He never responded to an offer I made to help recruit students. Perhaps he was afraid that I would try to recruit the "wrong" students. As I left his office, he thanked me.

Within my first few weeks at DePauw, some members of the department became concerned that I was too visible. One of them, Bob Eccles, said he couldn't remember any new faculty becoming a cause célèbre so fast and being so quickly identified with race problems on campus. Bob King worried that my talents as a teacher would be undermined or diminished by my focus on race problems. When I suggested that this was not his concern, he admitted that he was afraid the administration would try to stop the department from hiring me again next year. A third department member, Bob Newton, stuck up for me. He said he was delighted with what I was doing and I shouldn't stop. He said he'd waited ten years before he said anything critical about DePauw and that the administration still resented him for it, so it didn't matter at all that I was so new. What mattered was that I was critical about critical issues and wasn't afraid to make that known. (Bob Newton's wife, Ann, in another conversation, suggested that some in the department had a problem with me because I was a woman and I was smarter than they thought I'd be.) Russell Compton, our chair, was nothing but supportive and did not want me to be muzzled. I think I was more than naïve. I wanted to be judged well, and so I judged myself well and refused to see that others were alarmed or even repulsed by what I was doing. I tried to raise provocative questions in and out of class, and I didn't want to focus on the people who reacted so negatively to me. How could I have been so unselfconscious? I wanted to be provocative, yet I didn't expect or want to be the target of people's ire.

The world of DePauw was cloistered, with its tradition of sororities and fraternities and its homogeneous student body. Diversity was not a concept understood by the administration. In one of the letters I wrote to my parents I said that I felt like a warrior going into battle. I had decided that either the campus would rally round me or I would be fired. I was not going to sit by and watch as the school continued its retrograde policies. I didn't experience what I was doing or saying as arrogance, though it must often have come across that way. I would have called it idealism back then, or youthful enthusiasm, but whatever it was, it felt intense and necessary. There is no question that I consciously chose a destructive path, because that is exactly what I was trying to do: shatter some of the foundations that held DePauw up. I was coming on like a hurricane on campus,

Joy, a rather incredible DePauw student, once told me that I seemed to be trying to live what I taught. I've always thought it was essential for a teacher to be a model, not simply an intellectual interlocutor, and because of this view, I decided that I had to refuse to attend any social functions of sororities and fraternities. I'd read about the histories of these organizations and could not tolerate their legacy of hazing, exclusion, and racism. There were a lot of professors on campus who did not attend such functions but said nothing. Being who I was at the time, I decided I had to explain my position. I wrote a note to the sororities and fraternities saying that I regretfully had to decline their invitation since I did not believe in what they stood for: "If I attend your social function, it is tantamount to an acceptance of the Greek system. That I cannot do." I added that I would be happy to come and discuss my views.

My note was passed around from one housemother to another. Some students informed me that a common response among the housemothers was "Who does she think she is? She must have been rejected by the sororities at her college." Some of the Greek students were intrigued, some were angry, but as far as I could tell, most wanted to understand why I would take such a position, and so began my conversations with sororities and fraternities. My recollection is that most of these conversations started out in a hostile way but ended up with a great deal of understanding.

An event called White Awareness Week was scheduled for, I believe, October of 1968. A group of students had decided last spring that something should be done on campus to raise awareness of the problem of racism in America and at DePauw University. (I must have been wrong about the response to Dr. King's assassination when I came for the interviews.) The administration refused to help with any of the expenses associated with this project. Everything (speakers' fees, programs, posters, etc.) was planned, financed, and carried out by the students. It was really impressive.

One of the first speakers was Charles Evers, the brother of civil rights activist Medgar Evers, who was assassinated on June 12, 1963, by Byron De La Beckwith Jr. Evers spoke in Gobin Hall, the campus church, which was packed with students, faculty, and administration. He began by apologizing for his inadequate command of English, explaining both touchingly and with some rancor that he and his brother had not been able to have a full education. He continued by speaking of his life, what he was seeing in the country, and the responsibilities we should feel wherever we were in our lives. There was time for questions, and since a number of us were pushing the administration to commit to recruiting more minorities, I thought I would raise this issue with Charles Evers. I stood up and asked him to explain why DePauw ought to have a greater number of minorities on campus than they now had. There was some applause, some anger, even some laughter (a response I associated with the applause). A friend sitting next to me was looking around and whispered that President Kerstetter was sitting behind us and had just turned purple. (Kerstetter had a very expressive bald head, and when he got upset it turned all sorts of colors. I snuck a look and saw that his head was darker than I had ever seen it before.) I have no recollection of how Evers responded to my question or the questions of others, but I do remember that as we all left his presentation, the president seemed to purposely turn away so he wouldn't have to say hello. That evening some of us met with Evers to talk about the problems at DePauw and what we could do. Arguments broke out, and Evers was always the one to try and calm us down. He appeared to have a kind of serenity about him. I was sure he had impressed everyone. I was to find out that this was not so.

Later in the week, I was invited to dinner at one of the frat houses to talk about the problems of racism that we had been considering during

White Awareness Week. I arrived at the house and was met at the door graciously, if a bit formally. I was introduced to the housemother, a thin, gaunt, grey-haired woman, and terribly proper. I could not bring myself to call her Mom Toy as everyone else did, and she could not bring herself to ask me about anything but the weather. I was led into dinner on the arm of the fraternity president, which was strange to me and made me somewhat shy. Dinner wasn't exactly comfortable. The officers of the house were at my table (or I was at theirs), and they hardly seemed open or even cordial, although they usually smiled at every question and answer. The conversation at the dinner table centered on Charles Evers and their response to him. Essentially, they thought he was too emotional and not logical or rational enough. They also criticized him because his English was not perfect. They made no mention of the kind of person who emerged in his presentation, the way in which he showed us something below the surface impression he made. It seemed to me they were saying that any demonstration of feeling was "too emotional." He wasn't a theorist, he was an activist, but this was not something they respected or perhaps even understood.

I feared that dinner would never end, but it finally did and we proceeded into a lounge. I felt that they were ready for a kill and I was the enemy and so the target. I began with the excerpt from J. Saunders Redding that I read in the Basic Beliefs course, about his son Conway. I thought it would stir them, and it did, but to my surprise the first response was hostile (although I have to wonder why I was surprised after that dinner). One of the fraternity brothers looked at me and said angrily, "And that was supposed to prove what?" Deciding that I would try to be non-confrontational, I replied that it was not supposed to prove anything, only to reveal some experiences and feelings about part of someone's life. I kept trying to get these students to look at their own lives and their own feelings, but their anger was too great. They refused to see that they did not live in the immensity of the problem, that they lived in part of the problem at DePauw and in their own living quarters, and that they needed to think of problem solving on the scale of doing what they could where they were. It was not a successful meeting.

I was also invited to dinner by a sorority that I was told was the most reactionary sorority on campus. Although friends warned that I was walking into a lion's den and that they were out for blood, I went. After dinner, we convened in the living room—me and about fifty young women. I sat on the floor, as did some of them. Others sat on the couch, peering at me with what seemed a great deal of hostility. I tried to explain some of the history of secret societies like sororities and fraternities and how they were based on racist ideas. When I compared these ideas to Nazi ideas about race, the young women reacted in horror and suggested that my brains were in the wrong place. I kept saying that they were either ignoring or ignorant of the system they were in. I mentioned the tactic of "blackballing" and the deep racist roots of the word. I continued to describe the blindness perpetuated by sororities and the ideas bolstered by their presence.

After two hours of talking, something changed in the room. Even the women who had seemed so hostile got off the couch and joined me on the floor. They said that they had begun to understand what I was saying. Soon they were talking about their fears, how they were uncomfortable on campus, why they had joined a sorority, what they needed. All of a sudden, we became a group still in disagreement in some ways but able to listen to each other. We continued for two more hours, and then another change occurred, with some of the women expressing interest in organizing against sororities and fraternities. At that point I wished I could have hired Saul Alinsky, the firebrand community activist. I wanted to help, but I didn't have the tools or the experience. I guess my activism was limited.

Another sorority house wanted me to speak at their scholarship dinner. The adviser to that house was the wife of Louis Fontaine, director of admissions. She refused to accept me even as a possible speaker and warned that if the sorority sisters invited me, she would not set foot across the doorway—which she didn't because the sisters unanimously voted for me. My experience there was similar to what I'd encountered at other Greek houses, first hostility and then being able to talk with each other. The sorority asked me to come back for dinner, and their housemother even called me by my first name.

When I put up a resolution in faculty meeting congratulating the students for what they had accomplished in White Awareness Week and expressing hope that their efforts would not end with the conclusion of the project, the faculty in attendance applauded and voted unanimously to support the resolution. At this point I wondered if I could keep up the pace. Could I decide to stay here? Could I do more by way of changing things? Was I laboring under an illusion, or worse, a delusion? There was no doubt that I was having an impact.

I was soon asked to attend the meetings of the Student Council executive committee. I went regularly and once asked a question during a discussion of difficulties in raising money for fellowships and scholarships. Specifically, I asked whether these money problems might be related to the the lack of minority representation in our student population. With that Dean Farber blew up. He screamed that I was accusing the university of being racist, that this accusation wasn't true, and that I should keep my ideas to myself. This outburst was unusual for the dean, who wasn't the emotional type. The executive committee was incredulous, and two faculty members even apologized to me. Dean Farber eventually calmed down, but he never said a word to me.

Later I heard a story that seemed to explain the outburst. I was told that when Dean Farber and Assistant Dean Ling were driving home one day, Farber turned to Ling and asked, "What are we going to do with Ringelheim? The president doesn't like the way she talks to him." I was never told what Ling's response was, but this story, if accurate, may have accounted for Farber's response to me.

In the late fall of 1968, my father had a heart attack and I went home to be with him. (He recovered and lived until 1993.) When I returned to DePauw, wearing my black faux-fur coat, a bunch of students and friends on the faculty picked me up at the airport. Joy was amongst them, and I will never forget what she said: "I feel like we're bringing a panther back to her cage." That statement was so powerful to me that I began to think more seriously about leaving DePauw, but I wanted to consider the second semester of teaching. Thoughts of leaving DePauw seemed to be always in the back of my mind, but not always front and center.

In spite of all that was good in the Basic Beliefs course, I had difficulties with it. As I said, it was a team-taught course, and the ideas of my team members often collided with mine. I very much wanted to try my hand at an introductory course in philosophy. I asked the department whether it was possible to leave the Basic Beliefs team so I could teach introductory philosophy in the second semester. They agreed and asked that I teach two sections of the course.

I decided to teach it as a social philosophy course called Concepts of Prejudice. This issue of prejudice was important to me, and I thought it would also be important to the students. The problems of prejudice and oppression struck deep chords in me because of my identification with the history of my family and others. My parents had told me about their experiences in Europe. My father told me that his parents and younger brother were killed during the Holocaust. I met with many Jews who had been oppressed by the Nazis, and I developed a sense of guilt about being alive. Why had I been spared? This guilt did not remain an internal feeling. It turned into a need to understand why and how people could allow such horrors to be committed. I wanted to learn to act against those bolstering prejudice and oppression. I wanted to learn how not to become an executioner or a helper. When I was a graduate student, racism and anti-Semitism were at the very top of the list of what I wanted to teach, the same topics I mentioned when I was interviewed at DePauw. Now I was going to get my chance.

I put together a reading list that made sense to me even though the readings did not have any clear philosophical foundation. Still, the lack of such a foundation plagued me. Was this really a philosophy course? That question was the beginning of a long-term issue for me as a teacher. I became unsure of what it meant to do philosophy since the style and content of the courses I taught fell outside the bounds of traditional philosophy and evoked mistrust in many quarters. The Philosophy and Religion Department was perhaps the only department at DePauw that did not question whether or not I was doing philosophy. Some in the department debated content with me, but they were still the most encouraging department I ever had.

In each of the two sections of Concepts of Prejudice there were thirty to forty students. One section was composed of ten or so seniors who wanted to take what was essentially a freshman course, along with first-year students and a few students from the first semester's Basic Beliefs course. I wanted a buffer for the vulnerability I expected to feel in teaching the class, and these students were the friends I needed, although I worried that they might be troublesome in some ways. While they were highly motivated and intelligent, I knew from Basic Beliefs that they were often not as patient as this class might require. It might be complicated to satisfy the needs of all the students if "class" differences were lived out: between philosophy majors and non-majors, between younger and older students, between those who were more experienced and those who did not see themselves as inexperienced even if they were. Then there were the more obvious differences: Black and white, Christian and non-Christian. (There were three Black students in one section and one Jewish person, namely me, in each section.) I was pretty sure it wouldn't be a boring class, but I was not at all sure whether all of us could handle what might transpire.

I wrote out the syllabus and some program notes to communicate what I hoped this class would be. When I finished, I wondered how any of us would manage to read all the books I suggested, not to mention how I would manage to read all the assigned student papers. There was a lot of excitement about this course, and it felt crucial to me. I was also conflicted about whether to continue my life on this campus or leave. I think I had already made my decision to leave but wanted to wait some weeks before I made it public.

The first day of class arrived. I lectured that day about philosophical and pedagogical corruption. I first defined philosophy abstractly, as a discipline of conceptual analysis. Another way to say this, I told the class, was that philosophers tried to give a thoughtful rendition of experience. Philosophers tended to talk in abstract terms even about life as they knew it. While their abstractions often seemed removed from life, philosophers talked about issues that were meaningful to them, which did not mean that what they said would be meaningful to others. Hence some translation was needed if students were to understand. I cited what I thought were the big questions of philosophy as enumerated by Kant: What can I know? What ought I to do? What may I hope?

By philosophical corruption, I meant something positive, a dialectical change from old to new. The Adam and Eve story is a mythical model: a falling up to self-consciousness, not a falling down to sin—the beginning of a search for knowledge. The story of Socrates, as portrayed by Plato, is a story of who we might be outside the garden of Eden—namely, gadflies. The urge to reason is a form of corruption that forces us to reconsider ourselves and the world, to think critically about both and to be willing to change. As I write now, I think this kind of corruption may be a way to move from the familiar to the strange and from the strange to the familiar.

I went on to say that I wanted our class to try to deal with a problem that philosophers had hardly touched upon, prejudice. I said that I wanted them to learn to be independent, to care for themselves, to define themselves on their own terms—in essence, to become their own teachers and in turn learn to question and care for others. I wanted us to be full human beings in that class instead of separating the emotional from the intellectual. The course was an experiment for me. To illustrate my view of the classroom, I quoted from Suzanne K. Langer's preface to *Philosophy in a New Key,* in which she thanks her friends for their moral support and says they confirm for her "the truth of what one lover of the arts, J. M. Thorburn, has said—that 'all the genuine, deep delight of life is in showing people the mud-pies you have made; and life is at its best when we confidingly recommend our mud-pies to each other's sympathetic consideration.'"

We began our discussion, and it went well. After class, one young woman, Karen, came up to me almost in tears to say that she wasn't sure she could stay. I asked her to explain, but she said she couldn't just then. She eventually told me that she was a blue-blooded racist from Nashville, Tennessee, and she was afraid of the Black students in the class, not afraid that they might harm her, but she had been taught not to speak about anything significant in the presence of Blacks, and most definitely not problems of race. I felt sick to my stomach. I was not prepared for a reaction like this, and I didn't know what to say. I suspect I was trying to be objective and simply listen, but that didn't last long.

The class as a whole met three days a week, Monday through Wednesday, and was divided into groups of five on Thursday to discuss ideas that had come up in the larger class and to share the journals I'd asked them to keep. I chose most of the groups arbitrarily, but not Karen's. I put Jack (whose name tag, written by him, read "Black Jack") in Karen's group with a number of other students I knew I could count on to be direct but also constructive.

I thought I might come to these smaller discussions just for a few sessions, but I quickly found that I wanted to keep coming, and the students gave their permission. I seemed to be jealous of their time together, and I wanted to be there because I thought I would learn a lot. I simply could not stay away. In particular, I had a compulsive fascination to remain in Karen's group. At some point Black Jack told me that he and two other Black students had decided they weren't going to talk about racism in the larger class, only in the smaller groups, because they thought their silence might release some inhibitions. They intimated that when we came to anti-Semitism, I shouldn't talk either. I agreed.

The class discussions were interesting but not very provocative. The one provocation was Karen's journals. Although she wouldn't talk in class, she certainly talked in her journals, which were placed in the library along with everyone else's so that the students could see what was being said outside their own smaller groups. Karen wrote quite honestly about her upbringing as a blue-blooded debutante from Tennessee and her belief that so-called prejudice against Blacks was just that, "so-called." I could not have predicted that these journals would become talking points for all sorts of students who weren't taking the class. It seemed as if half the student body was going to the library to see what Karen and others had written.

The reading list for the course included Ralph Ellison's *Invisible Man,* William White's *Lost Boundaries,* John Howard Griffin's *Black Like Me,* Richard Wright's *Native Son,* Howard Fast's *Freedom Road,* and Charles Silberman's *Crisis in Black and White,* chapter 5, "The Problem of Identification." After a few weeks of class, a number of students said they were unsure what it meant to be a victim and to be an oppressor. They didn't see themselves in either role, which made them feel distant from the readings. Their comments gave me an idea. I recalled an experiment devised by Jane Elliott, an elementary school teacher in a small Iowa town, right after the assassination of Martin Luther King. She divided her third-grade class, all white, on the basis of eye color and told the brown-eyed students that they were superior to the blue-eyed students and would therefore enjoy special privileges. Then she watched with alarm as the students began to internalize the traits she had assigned them. I thought we might try to replicate that experiment in our class. I suggested that we retain our ordinary classroom format and proceed to discuss the readings as we had been doing, but with one difference: certain students would be designated as "oppressors" and others as "oppressed."

The day we tried it in the first section of the class, it didn't work at all. I was part of the oppressor group, and when we gathered together on one side of the room and excluded the oppressed from our discussion, they simply marched out the door in fury. The rest of us spent the remainder of the class trying to figure out what to do. We learned one lesson immediately: some confrontation between the two groups must occur or else the relationship between oppressed and oppressor would not emerge. But how were we to have this confrontation and under what circumstances?

I suggested that the oppressor group come to class the next day wearing some inconspicuous sign (I don't remember now what it was) so I could identify them clearly. Then we would turn to our regular discussion as if nothing had occurred the day before—except that I would not call on any member of the oppressed group. No matter what, I would ignore them. I began our next class by calling on Black Jack from the oppressor group. Lola, one of the oppressed, raised her hand, and I nodded at her as if to say that I'd call on her when Black Jack finished, but instead I called on someone else from the oppressor group. Lola looked bewildered but tried again, and again I called on an oppressor. Others in the oppressed group also raised their hands and were ignored. I saw them begin to look at each other in confusion, but they said and did nothing. No one left the room.

Pressure began to build, and Jim, another of the oppressed, shouted at me, "What the hell is going on?" I shouted back, "Shut up. Who do you think you are? We are having a discussion and I haven't called on you." Jim shot me a look that was both quizzical and furious. The students were not used to such behavior from me, and I certainly was not used to displaying it. Jim kept quiet for another few minutes. I wasn't sure how long I could keep this up without explanation, because I was as uncomfortable as the students seemed to be. Then Jim tried to talk again, and I shouted at him even more harshly. I said that if he didn't shut up, I would be forced to throw him out of class. When I started to get up from my chair to move toward him, he quieted down.

Now the entire room was brimming with anxiety. It was difficult to tell who was more unnerved, the students or me. I was beginning to feel awful about the amount of power and control I'd been able to wield, an overwhelming feeling close to abject fear. No one, including me, tried to undo the power dynamic I had established. None of the oppressors made the least attempt to whisper a word of explanation to the oppressed

Perhaps ten minutes before the end of class, I stopped and said I could not go on because what was happening felt like a bomb had exploded before me. I told the oppressed group about our oppressor decision following their walkout yesterday and asked them what they were feeling. They said that at first they couldn't figure out what was going on and that it was all very strange, but when they eventually realized they were being excluded, many of them decided not even to try to participate because it was clear there was nothing they could do. They became passive, and that scared them. They said that while they found my behavior inconsistent with what they knew about me, I was very convincing. That scared *me*. Deep down I think I knew that the power was attractive to me, something I was too afraid to explore. It seemed to me that the other oppressors might be feeling similarly, because they said they were frightened too, but not enough to step out of the oppressor role.

The bell rang, but we didn't move. We didn't know what had hit us. Fear, hurt, pain, confusion? We sat as if hoping that if we stayed long enough it would all go away.

The experiment made an impression, but I was afraid to continue with it. Instead of repeating it with the other section of the class, I decided simply to tell them what had happened. Though I thought it had been a successful experiment, I wondered about the ethics of it. It seemed to me a genuine lesson in how easy it was to become an oppressor or a victim and how easy it was for a teacher or any authority figure to use his or her power. In a way this was what I'd been after and what the students had been asking for when they said they had no experience of being oppressors or victims, but I feared that the emotions unleashed were so strong as to make any deep learning shaky, if not impossible.

Aside from Karen and her journals, and even during the oppressor/oppressed experiment, there was little controversy about racism during the early part of the semester. Our discussions were calm almost to the point of boredom, but it was the calm that preceded the storm around anti-Semitism.

Our texts for the next part of the course were Laura Hobson's *Gentlemen's Agreement*, Bernard Malamud's *The Fixer*, Max Frisch's *Andorra*, Elie Wiesel's *Night*, and Chaim Potok's *The Chosen*. I had asked one of the small journal/discussion groups to begin a conversation for the first twenty minutes of class, with everyone else listening before we opened the discussion to the entire class. We were to begin with our reading of *Gentlemen's Agreement*.

I was a little late for that first discussion. I ran down the hall and found that all the chairs were set up in a circle as usual, except that the only one left was inside the circle. A bit uneasy, I took it. Within a few minutes I couldn't believe what I was hearing. I felt that the words and sentiments being expressed could not be coming from the students I knew. There was Nancy, who had seemed so liberal, sensitive, and concerned about Blacks when we discussed racism in the United States and around the world. Yet on the topic of anti-Semitism she said, "Of course there are kikey Jews. They are more clannish than Christians.

The reason Jews become comedians is that they hate themselves and they get rid of that hatred by telling ethnic jokes." Someone else said that Jews were more miserly than Christians. The word "kike" was used over and over and over.

I felt surrounded, as in fact I was, sitting there at the center of everyone's gaze. I didn't say anything that day because I had agreed to remain silent about anti-Semitism after the Black students in the class told me they weren't going to talk during our discussions of racism. Instead I wrote down what the students had been saying in a shaky script. They kept going, joking about the phrase "Jew 'em down" as if it meant nothing. For fifty minutes, not one person in the room objected to such comments, which seemed like a torrential rain of horrible words that would never stop.

When the class was over, I needed to talk. I went over to two students I knew well, Martha and Joy, and asked if they realized the import of what had been said. Had they heard? Was this the way people talked? Was "kike" a common term for a Jewish person? Was "Jew 'em down" a common phrase? They saw how rattled I was and were concerned about me, but somehow they hadn't heard the comments as I had. A few guys in the class were standing nearby, and one of them said, "Aw, come on, Joan. You're being too sensitive. 'Kike' is only a colloquialism." I wheeled around and yelled, "Shit, when did 'kike' become a neutral colloquialism? How come you never used the word 'nigger' in class?" I told them all to get away from me because I couldn't guarantee that I wouldn't do something rash. I was really out of control, and certainly not in teacher mode. I seemed to be ready for blood, and they felt that, but not the reason for it. I had to stop talking to them for fear I might say or do something I would regret, and besides, I'd promised to keep quiet so the students would be able to say what they really felt.

I spent a terrible evening wondering what the next day would bring. We sat in a circle as usual, but I was no longer in the center. The word "kike" was again used repeatedly, along with statements about the problem with Jews—what had they done to deserve the kind of treatment they got? I lasted for about twenty minutes before I screamed, "Stop! What the hell is going on here? Don't you hear what you're saying? We talked about Blacks for three weeks, and not once did any of you use the word 'nigger,' yet in a day and a half 'kike' has been used dozens of times. You don't know anything about prejudice. You only know that there are certain things you shouldn't say or think about Blacks because you've been *told* they're wrong, but you don't really understand."

I'm sure my outburst alarmed the students. Not only was it not what usually happened in a classroom, I didn't think it *should* happen, yet I couldn't help myself. Although they knew I had strong feelings, they had never seen me so vulnerable and upset. We began to talk about what they'd been saying and what they apparently couldn't hear. One girl said I was just different, which made me so angry that I left the circle and began to pace up and down the room, asking in a taunting fashion whether it was my walk, my clothes, my talk—what was so different? She said she didn't know, she just sat in her chair with a look that was neither nasty nor cruel, just baffled. Someone else asked if I was angry at them. Did I hate them? Did I blame them? "No," I said, "I can't blame you because you were brought up in a painfully ignorant world." It occurred to me that my extreme response was a result of feeling as if I had been a fly on the wall of rooms I had never been allowed to visit except through books. In my own way I was as ignorant as they were. I apologized for coming across so strongly, for allowing what was inside me to pour out, which wasn't fair to them given my role as their teacher. At that point our study was no longer books but ourselves. Some of the usual separations in classrooms were breaking down, and part of me knew that was a good thing, although I was beset by the usual questions: Was this teaching? Was this philosophy? How would I know?

When I finished my apology, Michael looked at me and said, "Teach us,

Joan. Teach us what we don't know. Teach us the history." I was more than surprised, because I knew the students had some education about the history of racism, but it hadn't occurred to me that they knew nothing of anti-Semitism. I agreed to present a short history of anti-Semitism at our next class, knowing I would have to grapple with all that had occurred this semester. Could I unite passion with reason? I wasn't sure what I'd started or what the end would be.

I was to give the lecture on a Monday. The weekend before was tense for me as I thought about what to say and what the effect would be. It was not going to be easy since I really loved these students. I went back to all the books I'd read about anti-Semitism and finally decided that I had to address its Christian roots. I spent my weekend with Raul Hilberg, Jules Isaac, Peter Hayes, and a few other Holocaust historians, trying to construct something that would make sense out of two thousand years of history in an hour. On Saturday afternoon I had to go for a walk. On Monday I would face both sections of the class, seventy to eighty Christian students who were going to hear some material they'd never heard before and might not even believe. I knew that what I would say would inflict great pain. I had a responsibility to this class, yet I feared that the truth might destroy any trust they had in me. I also wondered what I'd gotten myself into. Did I have to poke at hornet's nests? Why did blood have to boil? Tears have to flow? Pain have to be revealed? Was this what it meant for me to teach? Did I have a right to do it?

Monday came, and I uneasily stood at the front of the room and began to lecture about the history of anti-Semitism. I said that we needed to come out from the prison of our past, otherwise we were no more than victims or conspirators. Toleration based on ignorance was not toleration at all. I noted that we'd come up with the idea of this lecture because anti-Semitism was not dead—we'd experienced it in our class, or at least I had. Although we would look at anti-Semitism as it turned genocidal during the Holocaust, I refused to identify anti-Semitism only with Nazism. It did not begin or end with the Nazis. The Nazis were able to pick up on a cultural phenomenon in Western Europe and bring it to a so-called logical conclusion. There were reasons why the populace was so willing to accept policies against the Jews.

I suggested that one of the most important of these reasons was that the hatred of Jews lay inside the history of Christianity. What was it about the Western world that couldn't or wouldn't resist Hitler's racist policies? My major thesis was that the history of Christianity provided the warrant for the feelings, beliefs, and actions that culminated in the horror of World War II and the Holocaust. Without this history, there would have been no license for Hitler's actions in the feelings of the people of Europe.

I now see these statements as hyperbolic. I was clearly struggling for an answer that didn't lie in this history alone, which was just one link in the larger history. I didn't say this to the class because I wasn't aware of it at the time. I didn't see my own form of exaggeration.

I continued with my lecture. As far as I could tell, I said, there was very little if any Judeo-Christian tradition. Spiritual closeness had rarely characterized the history of these two groups. It seemed to me that the Jewish and Christian traditions were not divided by a hyphen but rather by pools of blood. As I reflect now, I'm sure that this statement really was hyperbolic. Was I saying it for effect? Perhaps.

I went on, saying that I wanted to discuss this history but I didn't pretend to understand the real reason for the virulence or the continuity of the hatred, which seemed to elude any clear, precise argument or explanation. I said I believed that Hitler (and Hitler types) were parasites who lived off of people like you and me, people who would not bomb churches, would not use the words "nigger" or "kike" if well trained (at least not in public). The real monsters of prejudice might not be the Hitler types. The real monsters might be those of us who were not so detectable, like Kathy in *Gentlemen's Agreement*. Here I quoted a passage from Hilberg's *The Destruction of the European Jews*.

> To summarize: since the fourth Century after Christ, there have been three anti-Jewish policies: conversion, expulsion, and annihilation. The second appears as an alternative to the first, and the third emerged as an alternative to the second. . . . The Nazi destruction process did not come out of the void; it was the culmination of a cyclical trend. We have observed the trend in the three successive goals of anti-Jewish administrators. The missionaries of Christianity had said in effect: You have no right to live among us as Jews. The secular rulers who followed had proclaimed: You have no right to live among us. The German Nazis at last decreed: You have no right to live.

I quoted a few more sources demonstrating the continuity of hatred of the Jews within the context of Christianity, and then I spoke about the origin of this hatred. We could begin, I said, with the apparent lack of Jewish acceptance of Jesus as the fulfillment of the Old Testament. Jewish resistance was a source of anger and apparent contradiction of some Christian teachings. This abstinence and obstinance of the Jews had to be explained. One of the explanations was that Jews were meant to be a warning to all—God would let the Jews live on in their willful blindness, outcast and universally rejected, as a lesson to those who denied Jesus. Jews were to be punished and serve as an object lesson for the rest of the world. And so began the teaching of contempt described in Jules Isaac's book of that name.

I explained that Isaac examined several particular teachings, including one asserting that Jews are collectively guilty of the crime of deicide (a teaching finally condemned in 1965 by the Second Vatican Council, and later by the World Council of Churches and the National Council of Churches), and another asserting that the dispersion and suffering of the Jews are proof that God is punishing them for killing Jesus and for their continual refusal to accept Jesus (though Isaac points out that the diaspora predated Christianity by five hundred years). The circular logic of the Church seemed to be that any bad treatment of Jews was a fulfillment of God's will and that the bad treatment proved the truth of divine punishment.

I went on to discuss some of the history of the centuries that followed the early years of Christianity, when Jews became not just strangers and recalcitrant nonbelievers but the killers of God. When attempts at mass conversion didn't work, the policy of ghettoization emerged, followed by the expulsions of the thirteenth through sixteenth centuries, with Jews forced out of England, France, Germany, Spain, Bohemia, and Italy. Myths sprang up, such as that the Talmud sanctioned the killing of Christians, with the result that Jews were blamed for the Black Death and accused of the ritual murder of young Christian boys.

Then I turned to the Christian Bible. I said that there was no reference to Jews as the killers of Jesus in the gospels of Matthew, Mark, or Luke, and that Matthew even says in chapter 26 that the Jews had nothing to do with the plot against Jesus. In John's gospel, he does seem to blame the Jews, but some scholars have pointed out that when he uses the words "the Jews" he is using a literary device to avoid repeating "High Priests and Pharisees," the people he really blames. If that is true, the Church Fathers paid no attention, hence Origen in the fourth century, who wrote, "The Jews nailed Christ to the Cross." I also cited anti-Jewish writings by St. Ambrose and St. John Chrysostom from around the same time, as well as much later examples concerning the myths of ritual murder and the mutilation of the consecrated bread (Pope Paul IV, 1555) and the writings of Martin Luther. And I used all this to make a comparison between canonical law and Nazi anti-Jewish measures. Church and popular doctrine over the succeeding centuries held that anyone who had persecuted, tortured, or massacred Jews had acted as an instrument of God. Hitler was not ignorant of this when he wrote in *Mein Kampf*, "I believe that I am today acting according to the purposes of the almighty creator. In resisting the Jew, I am fighting the Lord's battle."

I was coming to the end of my lecture. I said that the picture I'd painted was not complete because there was much that had happened in more recent times. For instance, it was not until the late eighteenth century that Jews were emancipated in France, and not until 1858 in England and 1871 in Germany. The Dreyfus Affair (1894-1906) revived anti-Semitism in France. In the early 1900s, a fabricated and widely circulated text called *The Protocols of the Elders of Zion* purported to show that Jews were plotting a world conspiracy to achieve global domination. In the 1940s and 1950s water fluoridation was portrayed as a Jewish plot. I said that in spite of all I'd left out, I had made my point: namely, that Nazism was not a momentary aberration but grew out of the fertile soil of anti-Semitism in the Western and Christian world. I ended by making a link between American racism and anti-Semitism. "Let me conclude," I said, "with a quote from Bernard Malamud's *The Fixer*:'There's something cursed, it seems to me, about a country where men have owned men as property. The stink of that corruption never escapes the soul, and it is the stink of future evil.' When," I asked, "will we remove the stink?"

The class sat there in silence. Some students looked angry, others looked bewildered, still others seemed to be wiping away tears. One student asked, "What did the Jews do to deserve that treatment? They must have done something to have such a history." Another student, Michael, said that he'd been ashamed to be white ever since he started to study racism and now he was ashamed to be white and Christian. We began to talk about guilt and shame, about collective guilt, about how it might be possible to change the world and what they could do themselves.

After the lecture, I wondered how I could doubt that this was a philosophy class. The questions raised were not imposed upon the material. As

Joy wrote, "These questions arose naturally from our study and were integral to it." They were not pushed on the students. They didn't matter because they would show up on an exam. They were our questions, part of our lives, and they mattered because we knew we had to answer them. We started out looking at the problem of prejudice and wound up asking the fundamental questions of every major field in philosophy: What is the nature of reality? The nature of humanity? How and what can we know? What is truth? What is the nature of moral reason and how do we make moral judgments? What is justice? What is the nature of legal and moral obligations and to what extent are they compatible? How do we decide between them if they are not compatible? What is a valid argument? What is the relationship between validity and truth? Can we know other persons? What, for that matter, is the status of the existence of other persons? To what extent are we free? What are the limits of rational argument? Why be responsible at all?

Bob King, my colleague in the Philosophy and Religion Department, attended the lecture in the afternoon section. He told me, "I came because I really doubted it was true that there were any Christian roots of anti-Semitism, but now I don't." Bob had a PhD in theology and had studied at Union Theological Seminary in New York. I wondered how he could be so ignorant of this history.

He suggested that I give the lecture publicly to the entire school. I agreed. About two hundred students showed up. A silence snuck into the lecture hall as I spoke, a silence that replicated what had happened in the two sections of my class. Since there was another meeting on campus that many students thought they should attend, there was no time for questions. Many left. Some remained and stared. It seemed as if the readings I offered up stymied discussion. When it was over, Michele, a Black student, ran up to me and began to cry on my shoulder. She looked at me and asked why we, Blacks and Jews, had to suffer so. Another student, John, a senior Philosophy and Religion major, walked out and never spoke to me again.

There were some weeks left in the semester. The prejudice class was still ongoing. On one occasion I talked with Karen in her journal group with Black Jack there. I said I admired her stamina and her efforts to get at truths about herself. She said she admired my openness despite her resistance to what I tried to say about the kinds of prejudice I saw her exhibiting. It might have turned into a screaming match between an apparent bigot and an apparent non-bigot. It didn't, but in spite of our age difference (I was twenty-eight, she was nineteen or twenty), I cannot claim that I was mature enough or experienced enough to say the right things or treat this young woman with sufficient support. I had to learn that my raw emotional responses were not always the best way to proceed.

But a week or so later, I did make a scene with Karen. I had been listening to her and reading her journals for some time, and that day I tried to question her. She had clear ideas about the place of Blacks. She had said that the man she married would have to be tested to make sure he didn't have any "Negro" blood. I wanted to make a dent in her self-proclaimed blue-blood status, conferred on her as a birthright and having nothing to do with what she did. I asked her what would happen if I decided to give her a D because she was a Southerner. The quality of her work didn't matter, I was going to give her a D just because of what she was. She seemed disconcerted but eventually said she thought that would be unfair. What right did I have to give her a bad grade because she was a Southerner? I said that was the rule I made up and asked if she would go to the administration to protest. She said she might since she didn't think any teacher had the right just to make up a rule. Then I asked her what would happen in her hometown if it was discovered that she had some "Negro" blood. Could she still go to the same parties and be friends with the same people? She said no, she'd be finished, her status destroyed. I asked whether she thought that was fair. Was she really any different? Would she pound on her friends' doors yelling, "It's me, it's Karen, I'm the same person"? I thought she was beginning to understand. The tears began to well up as Martha, Joy, Tom, and Black Jack sat there quietly and sadly. "Would you say that was unfair?" I demanded again. "Yes!" she screamed, and then I said, "Don't you see that's what you're doing to Blacks when you decide who and what they are on the basis of color and myth?" Quiet overcame us all. Had there been a breakthrough? Perhaps. Later Karen left me a note she'd been given by her roommate.

> From what you and other members of the class have said, your professor is guilty of the very thing of which she is accusing you, K. She is attacking a long established and proud culture with you as a scapegoat, and using techniques quite unworthy of a truly Christian person. She has taken a naïve girl entirely lacking in self-confidence and put her on display as an oddity (as well as members of your discussion group) and used brainwashing techniques of pressure, fear, and confusion to try to change in one semester the very core of your personality which has been developing for twenty years. Oh, I'm not saying this excuses you; quite on the contrary, I agree that a change in you will have to occur for your own happiness and wellbeing in our currently changing society. But a successful change will only come through patience, understanding, reasoning, and experience. The change in you was coming along well, in a healthy, natural way with the honestly concerned, discreet help of your friends like J, your sisters, and professors like Dr. E. But your philosophy professor's current methods are making a total physical and psychological wreck of you, K. No one can knock that foundation out from under a building and expect it to stand. That is trying to play God! That's asinine! And that is what she is trying to do!

This note shook me. I'd already had worries about whether I was on a power trip, about discipleship, about the ethics of what I was doing in the classroom. Karen had added a note of her own: "I think my roommate is right in saying the change in me was coming—slowly and surely. Too much was put before me too quickly; I cannot change overnight. This—if it ever really happens—will take months or even years. Basically I am a very unconfident individual; I must trust myself—be sure of myself—before anything concrete happens."

After Karen left the group that day, the rest of us stayed behind, attempting to calm each other down. We wondered if we had the courage to be her friend, which was what she needed. She couldn't let go of her whole tradition by herself. Soon we began to talk about problems in the class as a whole. There were antagonisms between the seniors and the other students. Few students were really participating, despite the discussion groups and the journals and my lectures. We thought that was irresponsible. Why didn't they take seriously what we were doing? Why was I still perceived as "teacher" in some old-fashioned way. At this Black Jack looked at me and said, "There are limits, Joan. You can't have all you want here. And no matter how hard you try, no matter how much you perceive the classroom as different, the majority of students are always going to perceive a separation between you and the class. There's nothing you can do about it." He was right, and I choked up. Karen was not the only one who had to face some truths. And Jack's comment also suggested that I should have treated Karen differently, in a more traditional teacher-student way. I had a romance about the classroom, and at that moment I realized painfully that I had failed to make it everything I wanted it to be—a consistent theme for me at the end of every course.

I thought back to the first semester when some friends and students picked me up at the airport after my father's heart attack and Joy said she felt like they were bringing a panther back to her cage. I hadn't really thought of leaving DePauw before then, but I'd thought about it since. I didn't feel like a panther, but I did feel caged. The landscape around Greencastle was flat and dull, there was but one movie theater in town, and good places to eat were scarce. The more I thought about this place, the unhappier I became.

I went to Russell Compton and said I wanted to leave DePauw. He invited me to lunch several times and tried to dissuade me. I told him I was afraid of what I might become. I felt that opportunities to grow and expand were too limited here and that I might grow tired too soon and lose my will to fight. I told him that I wanted a different social life, not only for male companionship but for the possibility of meeting all sorts of different people. I made it clear how warmly I felt toward him and the department, said I feared I wouldn't easily find a department or a chair who would be so good to me. I thought he understood, but I realized how wrong I was when he asked, "Can't you do what you want to do during vacations and remember those experiences during the year? Can't you have romances during the summer and live with that?" I could only say that I didn't want to live a life of memories.

During the second semester, I became part of the steering committee for a week-long symposium on human sexuality that would feature films, lectures, and meetings with students. One of the last events was to be a discussion between me and my friend Rose Levine, wife of Norman Levine in the history department. We had entitled our hour "The Open Bed Policy and Its Enemies." Originally, we had thought of giving a brief lecture followed by a discussion, but by the end of the week, we decided that the students didn't need another lecture and we would only have a discussion. When Rose and I walked to the front of the room that afternoon, having no idea how many would attend, we saw our two stools, a microphone, and a crowd of about six hundred students, faculty, and townspeople. We asked for written questions until the audience became comfortable speaking publicly. Rose picked out the first one and threw it to me: What does a female orgasm feel like? Thanks, Rose. While I have no clear memory of what I said, I'm pretty sure I resorted to metaphors. Rose said that my description was mine alone and that others might have different descriptions, and then she described matter-of-factly what an orgasm was like for her.

There was a hush in the hall, after which we had to continue taking questions without embarrassment or shyness to the best of our ability. We'd started at 4:00, and it was difficult to end at 5:30. After we finally concluded. Norman said that I reminded him of Rose when they were younger (Rose was now in her forties). As I recall, some of the male faculty and others in attendance were scandalized.

Meanwhile, another controversy was brewing and about to boil over. At a central location in one of the classroom buildings was a bulletin board known as the Opinion Board. One day a pornographic story went up on the board, and then someone put up a porno poem. The Opinion Board was now the Smut Board. The administration was more than incensed. I thought that if they had ignored the situation and done nothing, the board fuss would have subsided, but no, they posted a guard in hopes of catching the culprit or culprits. No one was caught. More and more "offensive" stuff went up on the board. The moral outrage of the administration and some faculty was un-believable. One might have thought that World War III had erupted in Greencastle.

A school-wide meeting was soon scheduled for the ballroom. About a thousand people came. During the discussion not one faculty mem-ber spoke against the administration's position that using the board for pornographic purposes was the beginning of the moral degenera-tion of the university. The administration had never spoken out against racism, poverty, or any issue of substance. I had to say something. I si-lently rehearsed while sitting there, counting to twenty to relax myself. When I was ready, I raised my hand. A hush came over the audience. Was it because a faculty member was going to speak? Or because they felt that I would say something to enrage the administration?

I began by saying that I was upset by what I was hearing. On the stage were some student leaders who smiled at me a little. Then I noticed that the university's vice-president, Norman Knights, had begun to move the pen he was holding in and out of his mouth as if it were a jackhammer. (I could easily do some Freudian analysis here, especially given the topic of the meeting, but I will refrain.) I said I found it embarrassing that this small matter had caught the moral imagination of the administration. It seemed to me that we needed to think hard and seriously about the reordering of our priorities. Surely, we ought not to be reduced to fretting over four-letter words. Did we really believe that this ought to be the major concern of a fine university? It was not this so-called Smut Board that spelled out the trouble we were in, and I hoped that we could get back to the real business of the university. When I sat down there was deafening applause, but as far as I remember, nothing changed and the controversy over the Smut Board died down as people grew bored by it all.

It was time to be open about my resignation. When I talked with a few students once I had finalized my decision with Russell, they were a bit stunned and told me that I was needed at DePauw and I owed them something. They wanted me to stay. I recalled some questions I was asked at the beginning of the first semester: Why did you come here? How long will you stay? There was a kind of intimacy at DePauw that provoked questions like this, questions I was never asked when I first arrived at other schools. However much I criticized DePauw, I had to face an important fact about the place: namely, that it meant so much to these students that they felt I was abandoning them. I think they understood my decision, but I felt a great deal of pain in these discussions. I wondered if I had let them down, and myself as well. As I said, I loved these students. I couldn't help but feel both heartbroken and comforted by my decision to leave.

I wrote a letter to the students about why I was leaving, a version of which ended up being published in the school newspaper. I needed to explain my position to anyone who might be interested, and this letter proved to be the easiest way to offer my reasons and feelings. I had resigned without having another job, but I was interviewed by Northeastern University in Boston about a month before I left DePauw, and they made an offer that I accepted.

There were responses to my letter about my leaving DePauw. I was thanked by some faculty, wives of faculty, and students. One particular dinner invitation demonstrated to me that my reasons for leaving were vindicated.

At about the time we were beginning to discuss anti-Semitism in the Introduction to Philosophy class, Ann and Bob Newton invited me to dinner. Though they were friends and had been supportive of me in many ways, I did not feel entirely comfortable with them and couldn't figure out why. There was something restrained in them, as in so many I met on campus. The restraint always frightened me because I sensed some kind of dishonesty going on beneath the surface.

We sat down to dinner. As the food was put on the table, I noticed the platter of meat and found myself wondering about it. I must have had a strange look on my face, because Ann said, "You're not kosher are you?" When I said no, why did she ask, she responded, "Well, this is ham and I wanted you to know." I tried to remain calm. I did not keep kosher, and I never intended for anyone to think I was religious in any way, but there was something in the air that was profoundly offensive. I looked at her and asked why she chose to mention this now rather than over the phone when she invited me. She looked back at me and smiled. "Well, I didn't think you'd mind," she said. "I thought you would eat it anyway." My calm evaporated, and I lashed out: "If I were kosher, I couldn't eat it, don't you understand? If you came to my house and I knew that you were observant about the rules against drinking in your church, I wouldn't serve liquor at all. And if I were observant of the rules of kosher as a Jewish person, your serving me ham would be an insult. As it is, it's still an insult even though I am not observant." The children at the dinner table, a ten-year-old boy and a fourteen-year-old girl, sat in bewilderment. The girl asked what kosher meant. I tried to explain while suppressing my surprise that she didn't know. Her father had a PhD in theology from Union Theological Seminary in New York, and her mother had a master's degree from the same place. They had lived in New York for some years and often taught the Hebrew Bible. In the Philosophy and Religion Department they were our experts on the Old Testament. The conversation went on until almost three in the morning, but I never found anything beneficial in it. I pushed the Newtons about the kind of insensitivity they seemed to demonstrate. I said that they only taught the Jewish religion through what they called the "Old Testament" and never with the use of Talmudic sources. Worse, the "Old Testament" always seemed no more than a preparation for the "New Testament," so they really weren't teaching Judaism at all. When I went home, exhausted, I remember thinking that perhaps they had learned something but knowing that I had.

I left DePauw wondering if I could replicate what I'd had there. DePauw was a kind of perfect storm for me. I suspect one's first year of teaching is always memorable, for good or ill, but for me there was something unique about DePauw, and perhaps about me as well at the time. I went there knowing that I was going to be provocative on campus. I'd read a great deal about Greek life, and I understood that I was going to be on a campus where racial issues would be problematic at best. Still, I had no idea that I would take such a robustly active role on campus, no idea that I would choose to be as provocative as I was. It was as if something took over and there was no way to stop it, or to stop myself. I suspect that if the students and some faculty had not responded to me as they did, I never would have proceeded as I did. I felt lonely and lost, but I also wanted to stir the place up. From the very first, I didn't want to be just another new professor. I wanted to make an impact, and even if I hadn't wanted to, something about the campus description of me was going to resonate. After all, wasn't I "the Jewish woman philosophy professor from the East Coast"? That aside, I was out for bear and took every opportunity I could to provoke, but in all honesty, I didn't do this only for the sake of provocation. I was deeply concerned about the issues that prompted me to comment and act. I very much wanted my students to pay attention to where they were and what was going on. I was genuinely concerned about the students and the school. I wanted them both to be better.

And so I refused to go to social events at sororities and fraternities. I spoke up at gatherings with administrators who were shortchanging students and pursuing racist policies. I spoke up at faculty meetings in the hope that the faculty would change. I constructed my classes around topics and a pedagogy that would give students the genuine freedom to learn. There is no doubt that there was much arrogance and self-aggrandizement in my behavior, even if it was unconscious at times. There is no doubt that I reacted extremely on a number of occasions and gave up my "distance" as a teacher. Perhaps I was more comfortable than I should have been with students. Sexual relationships were not for me, but I became close friends with many students, and perhaps that was too problematic for them.

In 1976, seven years after DePauw, I was still reflecting on my experience there. In a letter to my close friend Sally Hanley, I wrote, "Philosophy could be seen as a way to run from feelings, as a way to use one's reason so that the world becomes ordered in a way it never is in one's everyday life." I said that my need to become a philosopher in the first place was in part a need to be controlled and reasonable, "not this loud, unfettered thing I often felt like who flew off the handle and got upset," but that I had been trying to move away from "that control and that distance from real everyday life." I quoted John Dewey: "Philosophy recovers itself when it ceases to be a device for dealing with the problems of philosophers and becomes the method, cultivated by philosophers, for dealing with the problems of men." In the classroom more than in other places, I wrote to Sally, "I was willing to take the chance to be myself, less hindered by controls, less afraid," to be both personal and intellectual, to try to demonstrate the need to dissolve the mind/body, reason/emotion dichotomies and simply be persons. "This is part of the human dilemma brought into the class-room in the hopes of relinquishing it for something else that has to be better."

Was it better? I'm not sure about my success at DePauw. Joy wrote in a journal entry toward the end of the semester that I had seemed to think change would come quickly but finally understood that change needed time and patience. "Can we affirm one another?" she asked in conclusion. "Can we trust ourselves enough to believe that our individual perspective is worth giving, can we trust others enough to believe that they want and need it? And most of all, I suppose, do we want to?"

Michael responded in his journal with an apology to the class, which he read aloud at my request, as Joy had read hers.

> I'd never thought of the class as working together, working to help each and every individual toward an understanding of prejudice. . . . I'd never been in a class like this before. Always individual work was the key thing—working to understand and get the grade. . . . I can see that I was looking at the discussions of the class entirely out of perspective. Instead of working with you, I was placing myself away from you, but leaping like a vulture on any fruits of your labor that was of use to me. So I used the class entirely to my own benefit, never thinking that possibly I had a responsibility to do something in it to benefit others, rather than just myself. So I'm sorry, sorry for waiting to work with what you've done instead of working with you to accomplish something. I have thus far failed you. I can only hope that in the remaining three weeks, I can add 1/100 as much to the class as you have added to me.

Was this not success of some kind? Perhaps, but all the students in Concepts of Prejudice (known in the university's catalogue as

Philosophy 101b) had to write a self-evaluation, and I include two here, the first from Karen.

> All in all, I feel that I have grown a lot in this course. While I still remain just as prejudiced as before (if not more), my views are now greatly broadened. I have heard the arguments for the other side. Much to Joan's disappointment I am sure, I feel that I can now argue my side a little more effectively. It is too bad the semester is over, for I could shock people in the class (those who don't know me) with my opinions. But . . . despite all the frustration . . . I more or less thank Philosophy 101b for the opportunity to hear the other side and for building a foundation—although weak—for learning to "think." Perhaps this is more important for me than to be more familiar with the question of prejudice.

The second evaluation is from a student named Steve, who hadn't had much to say in the course of the semester.

> I consider it a privilege to have taken your course and to have known you, though only on a superficial level. Social Philosophy 101b will not be forgotten with the ease and the inevitability that other courses so often are. . . . Joan Ringelheim has definitely left her mark: she has affected everyone, from the commonest of students to the highest of the administrative force; because of her there emanates every kind of feeling from bitter resentment to loyal fidelity. . . . Her admirers are many; her enemies are many too. . . .
>
> I can think of many pertinent words to explain my personal assessment of myself in the class: expanded, aroused, provoked, challenged, puzzled, tumultuous, anxious, searching, pulsating, gratifying, intimidating, and absorbing. The course was characterized by unyielding personal entanglement and persistent

scrutiny and research and intellectual vitalization. I have never, all at once, been so intricately enmeshed in school work but so outwardly outcast in the school room. I felt detached and isolated in our interpersonal relationships so far as the group and whole class was concerned; however, I also felt real inner satisfaction as far as my individual investigation and inquiry and interest were concerned. This seems to be quite paradoxical, as indeed it is; class irritated me while the work intrigued me; as my attendance fell my involvement heightened; as my opinion of Joan lessened, my opinion of the course increased.

I never clashed with Joan for fear of my grade; but, regardless, she and I never got close because I never made the effort and didn't want to. I was progressively angrier with her because she continually degraded and criticized my every statement, my every journal, to the point of frustration. . . . My tacit discrimination against her, as I look back, seems immature and it was I think; for the first time she acquainted me with intrinsic intellectual conflict—a thing I have never really experienced. . . . In short, the course, with its independence, abstractness, intensity, and depth, was a valuable stepping stone in growing up for me. . . . there is no question in my mind in regard to its overall value to me as an individual. I gained in ways that can't be put down on paper. . . .

Joan Ringelheim introduced the lucky few who had her to a new dimension in education, and unfortunately some of us were just too conditioned to the "old" system to fully take advantage of her. I tried, and in my eyes I succeeded though in hers I may have stagnated. She forced me into a growing experience which I have not appreciated until now. And despite my personal prejudices against her, her insight and dedication and individuality overwhelm me.

When I left this class on prejudice for the last time, I felt full yet frightened. What would happen now? Could I continue to teach the way I taught at DePauw? Would I be criticized? Fired? Would I be able to re-create what we had at DePauw, or was that to be a unique experience? Could I communicate with the students at another school? I would soon see that DePauw would become a model for what would happen or not happen at other schools as I continued the course on prejudice under the title Prejudice and Oppression. This course, the method and the content, became the focus of attention everywhere I went. And the question that consistently pursued me in the class was the one that Joy put to me once: "What do you want of me, Joan?"

I left DePauw because it felt too small for me, yet what I found elsewhere were other forms of smallness. My teaching experience at DePauw remained a touchstone for me. At other universities I had some great classes and some wonderful students. In all the classes I taught after DePauw, it was as if everything—the readings, the discussions, myself, the students, their ideas and feelings—was a laboratory for philosophical analysis. Looking back, I hope that I did no lasting harm to students like Karen and Steve who were challenged by my approach. I allow myself to think that I did more good than harm in opening minds, not least my own.

THREE

The Holocaust and Women in the Holocaust

The Holocaust shaped my life, both personally and professionally. I did not experience the Holocaust directly: I did not survive a ghetto or a camp; I did not escape from Europe before or after the Nazis took over; I was not in hiding; I was not in the resistance against the Nazis. I was born in the United States. My involvement with the Holocaust is secondhand. I am a historical visitor, but not a casual one.

My mother and father, Anne and David, were born in Poland, Anne in 1910 in the city of Siedlce, my father in 1906 in Dubiecko. Anne's father died when she was six years old; she came to New York City with her mother and a sister when she was eight, joining five older brothers who had emigrated earlier, apparently in order to avoid being drafted into the Polish Army after the outbreak of World War I in 1914. When I was younger, I thought this was a terrible reason to leave Poland. Sometimes I thought that they must be cowards. I now wish that I had talked with at least some of them. I really never knew their stories, and I was too quick to make a negative judgment. On the other hand, why didn't they tell me? I remember that my mother specifically asked one of her brothers to tell me about their family and their life in Poland, but he refused. I have no idea why.

My mother was not a survivor of the Holocaust, nor did she have relatives who were murdered by the Nazis or their accomplices, at least as far as she knew, but she did tell me about a pogrom she experienced in Poland with her mother when she was six or seven. I was a young teenager at the time, and she painted a vivid picture of running away with her mother and hiding in the woods to escape the Poles chasing them. Her story made a deep impression on me, even though I found it difficult to imagine such circumstances.

When Anne finished eighth grade, her brothers coerced her to go to work, saying that a woman did not need an education beyond the eighth grade. She did not rebel against this decision, nor did her mother object. I believe she ended up working as a secretary for a number of years at a branch of the Vim Motor Truck Company.

David left Poland in 1924 when he was eighteen, along with his brother Sydney, then seventeen. Their parents, Miriam and Jacob, and two other siblings (Claire, born in 1911, and Josef born in 1921 or 1922) remained in Poland. Jacob had emigrated many years earlier and had become an American citizen in 1903, but he didn't like the United States, or so I gathered from family stories, and he returned to Poland in 1904 or 1905, marrying Miriam Reich soon after. He came back to the United States in May 1916 because of a violent incident at the flour factory he owned with his brother-in-law, Nathan, when they were attacked by one of their workers whom Nathan shot in the leg. Jacob had a gun too, and though he didn't shoot, he was the one to leave for the United States, perhaps because he was already a citizen. Apparently he still hated the US, because he later returned to Poland once again.

After years of living in their new homeland and becoming citizens, Anne and David met in New York at a dance, probably in 1932 or 1933. My father always claimed she danced very close to him that night, which led him to think she was attracted to him, but it seems she was dating other men at the time. My parents used to tell the story of my father keeping my grandmother company while he waited for Anne to return from a date. I have no idea how long this went on.

Anne and David married in 1935, and by the time I was born in 1939, they were living in Bridgeport, Connecticut. Along with my father's brother Sydney, they had moved to Connecticut to set up the Globe Equipment Company, established in 1938 to provide equipment to restaurants in the Connecticut area. David and Sydney had been working with Benjamin, a brother of their father's, selling restaurant supplies in Lower Manhattan, but they probably thought Connecticut was a more viable place to start a business. My mother didn't work again until I went off to college, when she took a job selling women's clothing at Howland's Department Store in Fairfield.

As children in Poland, my parents had both been raised in a Hasidic Orthodox tradition, but they did not remain observant Jews. They were members of a conservative synagogue in Bridgeport and observed some holidays, but my brother and I were not raised in a religious Jewish household. We had ham and bacon in our refrigerator, foods that did not conform to Jewish dietary laws and therefore were not kosher. Even so, I remember that we never had milk at dinner, and when I went off to college at Oberlin Conservatory, I was surprised to see milk on the dinner table. In a religious Jewish household, one would not have milk with meat. It was uncomfortable for me even to see the milk, not because I was religious, but because I just wasn't used to it.

I went to Hebrew school, as did my brother, Ted, but when I told my parents that I wasn't learning anything there and wanted to leave, they acceded to my wishes. Ted wanted to have a Bar Mitzvah (a Jewish coming-of-age ritual for boys, called a Bat Mitzvah in the case of girls), and my parents very much wanted him to have one. I remember my father spending time with Ted going over the Torah portion he was to read at the service. My brother often opened up the ironing board that was built into the kitchen wall, laid his Torah portion on it, and read the Hebrew words to my father. For myself, I never wanted a Bat Mitzvah, and that seemed to be fine with our parents, maybe because of gender—a boy needed a coming-of-age ritual but a girl didn't? Or perhaps they simply believed me when I said I wasn't getting anything out of Hebrew school. In any case, neither of my parents seemed too concerned with what it meant to be Jewish in any religious sense. Still, a sensitivity to anti-Semitism played a large role in my growing up in this household.

When I was in sixth grade, in 1949, I found it problematic that Christmas was acknowledged and celebrated while Chanukah was ignored. That didn't seem right to me, and I said so. The disagreement about this in my classroom became so vehement that the teacher allowed us to separate our desks into two groups on either side of the room, one for each viewpoint. I don't remember whether the teacher did anything beyond letting us change the classroom's seating arrangements, nor do I have any memory of which side "won." Today I regret that the holidays of groups other than Christians and Jews played no role in our protest. At that point, I was sensitive to anti-Semitism and to a lesser extent racism, but not to other prejudices or oppressive behaviors.

At my middle school graduation in 1952, I was chosen to speak some introductory words on behalf of my class. The class, in turn, was sup-posed to read in unison from a text they had written or chosen. I found the use of the term "black" in their text problematic, and I protested it. (My memory of this text is very hazy, but I think it was referring to the variety of Americans in the United States and not to race per se as an issue. Still, I wonder now whether it was so innocent.) I thought "black" was insulting, harsh, and simply negative. I lived in a white world and had no idea how much debate was going on in the African American community about what terms to use. I mention this because it reflects my interest in racism as a young person, as well as the level of naïveté that surrounded my ideas at the time. It also demonstrates how little the concerns of the African American community penetrated the consciousness of so-called liberal whites like me.

When I became interested in getting a summer job in 1953 or 1954, my mother told me that the bank to which I was applying probably wouldn't hire me because I was Jewish. I don't remember how I reacted to what she said, but I never forgot that she said it.

In high school, when I learned that the Daughters of the American Revolution had never given their citizenship award to a Jewish student, I immediately decided to win it, and in my senior year, I did. I probably won only because the high school faculty outvoted the DAR members, but it didn't matter to me very much because the award still belonged to me, a Jewish girl of eighteen.

I first met survivors of the Holocaust when I was nine or ten. These were social occasions, and the survivors were friends of my dad's sister, Claire. She had been living in Pisa, Italy, with her husband, who had emigrated with a group of Polish medical students forbidden to study in Poland because they were Jewish. He and the other students returned to Poland after the Germans attacked in 1939, and he was shot along with all but one or two of his colleagues. Claire also attempted to return to Poland but could not. She came to the United States in 1941 or 1942 and eventually remarried.

I remember the tension and fear I felt when I met survivors; I never asked any questions. I didn't know what to think, couldn't figure out what questions to ask. Much later, when I was in college, Claire told me about her first husband, the Polish medical student killed by the Nazis. I had already learned that some eighty members of my father's family had perished in the Holocaust.

The silence around the Holocaust in my family remained a mystery to me for a long time. I was twelve or thirteen when my father told me that the Nazis had killed his mother, father, and youngest brother in Bergen-Belsen. I don't remember what prompted him to tell me. It wasn't until after college that I met and talked with survivors on my own and began to reflect on the ways in which the Holocaust might have affected Claire and my father. It took much longer for me to reflect on the impact the Holocaust had on me, and to this day I'm still working it out.

It strikes me now that I never asked my father a single question about the killing of his parents and youngest brother. Bergen-Belsen was in northern Germany, and it would have been more than unusual for Polish Jews to be sent there; most Jews in Poland and all over Europe were sent east to Auschwitz and other camps in Nazi-occupied central Europe. Nor did I ask my father for details about the killing, whether they had starved to death or been gassed or shot. Even after I knew a great deal about Holocaust history, I did not want or was unable to think about the factual information he had given me. I suppose it startled me so much that I didn't want to raise any questions with him, or with myself. I simply accepted what he said because there seemed to be no reason to do otherwise. Only when I was in my fifties, after I started working at the United States Holocaust Memorial Museum, did I begin asking questions, but not of my father. I was talking with a relative by marriage of Claire's second husband, and I asked her if she knew anything about what had happened to my grandparents and my young uncle. She didn't, but she gave me the name of a woman with firsthand knowledge, and that woman told me that they were shot at Sambor, a Jewish ghetto established by the Nazis in Ukraine, and not killed at Bergen-Belsen. She said they were on their way to Moscow to get papers to come to the US—since Jacob, my father's father, was a US citizen, there would be no question about quotas—but they never made it to Moscow. They were caught by the Nazis in Sambor and shot along with other Jews.

I told my father what I had found out one day as we met with some mutual friends. I was angry at him for not telling me the truth or not knowing the truth or not pursuing it. I actually yelled at him, but as I recall, all he said was, "Oh." He never chastised me for my outburst, and I'm still not certain where my anger came from. Often I think I was angry at myself for not knowing or not thinking through what my father told me, angry that I waited so long to find out the specifics, but it made no difference to my dad—his parents and his youngest brother were dead, and the facts didn't matter.

As I said, survivors frightened me at first, and this fear continued throughout my high school and college years and beyond. I remember being afraid that they might have done something terrible in order to survive. Now I suspect that I didn't want to hear how awful it was for them because it was too much for me. Consciously or unconsciously, I must have wondered whether I could have survived in their circumstances or whether I would even have tried.

I was on the staff of the US Holocaust Memorial Museum in Washington, DC, from 1989 to 2007. The museum opened in April 1993, and when I was diagnosed with breast cancer that June, I remember saying to myself that I wanted to have cancer. Though I told this story to friends over and over, I never really thought about the complexities of my response until the last few years. It never occurred to me at the time that it might have to do with my guilt or shame because I did not experience a ghetto or a concentration camp, or that it might even be a form of PTSD.

It was doubtless because of my family's history and the people I encountered growing up that the Holocaust became important to me. My interest was not shared by my Jewish or Christian friends in high school or college, nor was it an academic subject in college or graduate school. When I wrote a dissertation proposal on Hegel's concept of the hero and its possible relationship to Hitler, my dissertation committee didn't think the topic made sense and did not approve it. I ended up with a proposal on psychoanalysis and history.

Although I had no environment larger than my own family in which to think about the Holocaust, I was so drawn to it that in grad school I made a list of topics I wanted to teach once I received my PhD in philosophy, with anti-Semitism and racism at the top. I wanted to be able to connect the history of the Holocaust to the history of anti-Semitism, to use anti-Semitism as a way to understand the historical events of the Holocaust. I also wanted to teach about racism in America. I thought it essential to speak about some of the issues that were part of American history and culture but were not taught to most students. Racism and anti-Semitism and the Holocaust were not at all what most philosophers seemed to talk about, but I was persuaded by my own study that these were crucial topics that had to be addressed no matter how distant they might seem in contemporary philosophical circles.

If family history was what drew me to the Holocaust in the first place, I have no clear idea what kept me there. Attraction to horror? Identification with victimization? A type of survivor guilt? Did I think studying it and talking about it was a form of activism? Did the Holocaust as a study serve as a substitute for present-day responsibilities to stand against racism and oppression? It is easy to clothe yourself in moral garb if you work on the past. I am still not sure why my interest in the Holocaust was so obsessive, and perhaps even excessive to others.

During my first year of teaching, at DePauw University in 1968, my courses focused on racism, anti-Semitism, and the Holocaust. I did not come to feminism or feminist theory until around 1973, so the issue of gender during the Holocaust did not arise for me before then. Once I began to teach feminist theory in 1975 or 1976, I recall asking myself a simple question about the Holocaust: Where were the women? I had been seeing only men in the historical literature, and I began to wonder whether or in what ways the experiences of women replicated or were different from those of men. Did gender count in some way? If yes, how?

In the 1970s the Holocaust was not much of an issue for feminists, Jewish or otherwise. Many considered the Holocaust a narrow religious interest and a distraction from what was essential to feminist thinking. I didn't see it that way.

In 1978 I attended a conference on the Holocaust, and at the end of one session I vividly recall leaving in the company of two women I had just met, Helen Fagin and Susan Cernyak-Spatz, both survivors and both university professors, which was all I knew about them at the time. When I asked what I naïvely thought was my simple question—"What about the women?"—Helen Fagin did not hesitate for a moment. She stepped away, facing me, almost as if she were afraid to show me her back, and said in no uncertain terms, "I don't want the Holocaust to be made secondary to feminism." I practically shouted, "I have no idea what the question really means yet," but she was gone, so fast that you might have thought I had a disease. Perhaps to her I did. Now I had to think about whether the Holocaust transcended gender. Was it an event so unique that any ordinary categories of inquiry seemed senseless or even sacrilegious? This viewpoint would crop up in most discussions I had about the Holocaust and women, always difficult and wrenching discussions.

After Helen made her exit, I turned to Susan, who stayed to talk and proceeded to tell me that she was a graduate of Theresienstadt, Auschwitz, and Ravensbrück. I internally gulped at this revelation as she went on to say that sex didn't matter in the camps. I tried to explain that sex wasn't necessarily the primary issue, and we continued to talk throughout the day. She kept trying to find examples to demonstrate that studying women during the Holocaust was pointless because being a woman didn't matter, but the examples she related suggested a need for further study. For instance, she told me that women guards were more vicious than male guards. If so, why wasn't this something to pursue? Further, if she had been only in sex-segregated camps with female guards, how could she compare the behavior of male and female guards? And supposing that she had been able to observe both, did the women guards appear to be more vicious even when doing the same things as the men? Did the brutality of the women seem more vicious than that of the men even if the behavior was similar or the same?

By the end of the day, I was convinced that further investigation was warranted. It took Susan more than this one day to think that women during the Holocaust was a viable subject of study, but she did not run away like Helen Fagin. I don't think she ever changed her mind about the brutality of female guards. I kept mulling over the issue but did not pursue it in a diligent way with Susan before she died in 2019 at the age of ninety-seven.

At another Holocaust conference, in 1979, I found myself in an informal discussion with Yael Danieli, Eva Fleischner, Henry Friedlander, Raul Hilberg, and Sybil Milton. Except for Yael, all were noted scholars of the Holocaust in various fields of specialization. Yael, a therapist who worked with children of survivors, raised the question of why these children tended to fear that their mothers had been raped. She thought from her experience with them that this fear was widespread and that it might represent some reality.

Without hesitation, those of my colleagues who responded claimed that the children's fear was not based on actual incidents of rape but on fantasies induced by the media's sexualization of the Holocaust. I believe they were speaking of films and plays that focused on the importance of sex during the Holocaust, dramatizing the rapes of women prisoners, for example, or the uses of women prisoners as prostitutes, or the guards' interest in women prisoners sexually. No one cited any research; no one referred to any documentation or studies of interviews with survivors, male or female. No other issues were raised, no other questions posed. No one discussed relationships between women and children in the Holocaust. No one spoke about the possible relationship between gender and survival. No one talked about

German women as perpetrators or collaborators. No one discussed the structure of women's camps, women in resistance, women political prisoners, or the relationships of men and women, women and women, men and men. No one discussed the possible differences between ghetto life and camp life—in the former, women and men were together, and in the latter, they were not. There was no pursuit of the issue, just an immediate and resounding denigration of the question. No concepts were readily available to shape such a conversation; there was no historical road map. Feminist theory would have helped, but no one at the time was prepared to apply it to the Holocaust. As I remember that scene, I was silent, not knowing what to say, but the exchange is seared into my memory.

I soon began to pursue such questions on my own, the main one being whether we would understand the Holocaust differently if women's experiences were reclaimed and their voices heard. To that larger question I added a list of smaller ones: Did women survive better than men? What were women's survival strategies? Did women cope better than men? Were women's relationships with other women different from men's relationships with other men? Was women's resistance different from men's? What was the relationship between women and men in resistance? Did women and men have different roles? What were women's particular vulnerabilities?

When I first began to write about women and the Holocaust, it was clear that battle lines were going to be drawn, lines between those who believed such an investigation would trivialize the Holocaust and those who thought it might change or even revolutionize the study of the Holocaust. At an April 1982 Scholar's Conference on the Church Struggle and the Holocaust, sponsored by the National Conference of Christians and Jews, I gave my first paper on the topic, entitled "The Unethical and the Unspeakable." (The word "unspeakable" was a reference to those who thought the Holocaust could not be described in words, but "unethical" now seems to me much too tame a word for the atrocities committed during the Holocaust.) The paper was, I think, in the mode of cultural feminism, an assertion that women survived better than men and were somehow better than men in the circumstances of the Holocaust. I wasn't conscious of this perspective at the time, nor do I think the commentator, Michael Wyschograd, was upset by whatever my particular perspective was. He was only upset by my talking about women, no matter how I talked about them.

Wyschograd said that the most interesting part of the paper was my middle name, Miriam. It was my grandmother's name. As I've said, she had been murdered by the Nazis along with my grandfather, Jacob, and their youngest son, Josef. To honor her, I took her name as my middle name for a few years as I began working on the Holocaust, and I'm embarrassed to admit that I stopped using it because I didn't like how I wrote the letter M—a trivial reason, but perhaps less trivial than Wyschograd's assertion that my middle name was the only worthwhile thing about what I had to say. He thought that any work on women and the Holocaust was disrespectful. To him, there was no issue about women during the Holocaust, and certainly not from a feminist perspective, a view that became commonplace in the world of Holocaust studies. Larry Langer, a scholar of Holocaust literature, was also on the program, and I don't recall what he said at the time, but in subsequent years he was directly hostile to feminist ideas on the subject.

In this first paper, I began by suggesting that one could not simply assume that all survivors experienced the Holocaust in the same way. It was my position that the lives of women had been obscured or erased from Holocaust history. Women's experiences had been neutralized into a "human perspective" so that issues related specifically to women were excluded. I continued:

> At the very least, we must acknowledge the special abuse of women in sexual and parental roles, in gender-defined conditions and roles within ghettos, in resistance groups, and in

the camps. We need to define women's values and show how they helped shape their experiences. It is not so clear whether women's values were destroyed. The evidence [in the early stages of research] indicated that women's relationships with other women were significantly different from those of men with other men. Surely, we cannot overlook this and simply proceed to talk in the usual way about the isolation of prisoners from one another or the destruction of values. In order to find out why or whether it might be true that women survived better, we must look at the ways in which women construct survival strategies and meaningful choices in varying conditions of powerlessness.

Here I can now see the grounding of something of a cultural feminist view of women in this paper, a view I did not hold forever. Indeed, I changed my mind in a radical way when I gave a paper at the Berkshire Conference on the History of Women in 1984, as I will explain later on in this essay.

The idea for a conference on women and the Holocaust probably had its beginnings in my head in 1979 or 1980. After many applications for grants, the New York Council for the Humanities came through, and the first such conference, Women Surviving: The Holocaust, took place in Manhattan on March 20-21, 1983, at Stern College for Women of Yeshiva University. I directed this conference with Esther Katz, the conference coordinator, who was a child of survivors and received her PhD in history from New York University. (She is now a retired associate professor of US History at NYU and director/editor of the Margaret Sanger Papers Project.) More than four hundred people attended each day—we had expected half that or fewer. Since the auditorium could only hold so many, we had to turn a number of people away.

The conference was apparently seminal, even legendary, to some who were there, though of course it was not, nor could it have been, definitive. In a letter to me, scholars Atina Grossmann, Marion Kaplan, and Renate Bridenthal wrote, "It gave voice to women survivors and served notice to scholars that even during the extreme events of the Nazi 'Final Solution' ... gender mattered." We brought together people who didn't usually and probably still don't come together at Holocaust conferences: survivors, scholars, children of survivors, other interested members of the community, feminists of all kinds, and some twenty or thirty men. The combination was rich, if sometimes uneven.

This was a conference where scholars were not the center of attention; the survivors of the Holocaust were. The survivors were considered to be the experiential experts, and the scholars had to listen. There was very little scholarly analysis as compared with the personal stories of the survivors. The lack of scholarly analysis caused some unevenness in the conference and troubled some members of the audience who wanted more from the scholars, whereas some thought that the lack was the strength of the conference. There was no winning on this score.

If I had to summarize the conference, I would say that the three most important things were the emergence of personal stories, especially from women who didn't usually speak or feel that they could speak; some scholarly analysis in the field of women and the Holocaust, such as it was at the time; and most importantly, the raising of consciousness that women during the Holocaust had to be studied.

The conference was volatile. People had a lot to say. Participation was broad and unquiet, the findings were limited. There were fights among different ideologies and perspectives, perhaps the biggest ones involving feminists and lesbians who found it difficult if not impossible to listen to those who did not share their views. It was also clear that survivors had a very difficult time thinking about themselves as women and that many simply didn't want to do so. Still, there was something vital about this conference, something genuinely exciting and unpredictable. It was also tiring—I didn't sleep well for the next couple of weeks.

It might be useful to summarize my opening remarks, in which I began by criticizing the title of the conference: Women Surviving: The Holocaust. I suggested that those two words, "The Holocaust," always uttered as if written in stone, did not describe a single event, that what men and women and children experienced was not one event but a myriad of events that we'd tied into an analytical knot so we could speak about it in a single breath. I argued that "The Holocaust" was made up of individual experiences that we had no language to describe as people faced their particular circumstances. I said that not everyone experienced "The Holocaust" in the same way, and that at this conference we would explore differences between the experiences of men and women as well as differences among women's experiences.

I moved on to the term "surviving," which I found very problematic. It seemed to me that what women were doing was trying to survive, except that you only knew you were a survivor after the events were over. I said I wished that the conference was about women trying to survive so we didn't only talk about the ones who got through but also about all the women, all the people, who tried to survive but didn't make it. I suggested that we needed to reclaim the history of those who were here today as well as those who were not here, and that a better subtitle for the conference might be Women Maintaining Themselves, instead of Women Surviving.

I then moved to my last point: Why talk about women at all? Didn't that trivialize the Holocaust? If it was not trivial to write about one camp, one Judenrat, one person, I said, how could it possibly be trivial to talk about women? If we talked about the Holocaust only in terms of its sacredness and uniqueness, wouldn't that preclude us from talking about or hearing stories about life in the camps that might demonstrate ways in which women operated differently and perhaps transformed situations of death and impoverishment into possibilities for life?

I had invited the noted writer Cynthia Ozick to the conference, and her response serves to indicate the level of hostility that accompanied my work and the subject of the conference.

> I think you are asking the wrong question. Not simply the wrong question in the sense of not having found the right one; I think you are asking a *morally* wrong question, a question that leads us still further down the road of eradicating Jews from history. You are—I hope inadvertently—joining up with the likes of [the Revisionists] who [say] that if it happened to Jews it never happened. You insist that it didn't happen to "just Jews." It happened to the women, and it is only a detail that the women were Jewish. It is not a detail. It is everything, the whole story. Your project is, in my view, an ambitious falsehood. . . . The Holocaust happened to victims who were not seen as men, women, or children . . . but as Jews.

After the conference, I continued to interview survivors and tried to think through my research. I eventually realized that I was espousing a kind of feminist nationalism and valorizing women in a way that would only repeat the mistake of celebrating and glorifying the oppressed. My reading of Ti-Grace Atkinson's paper on female nationalism and my discussions with her brought me to see that my perspective on women and the Holocaust was too limited. It was this self-critique to which I turned in my 1984 paper at the Berkshire Conference on the History of Women. In what follows, I have condensed the paper to its main points and left most of it in the present tense, as it was when I gave it.

I began by saying that the Holocaust was a story of loss, not gain, not for anyone. I cited statistics on the deaths of Jews, most of them killed in Europe. In addition, one fourth to one half of the Roma population was killed, as well as some 250,000 homosexual men. The list goes on, I said. Even if we can find differences between women and men, even if women did maintain themselves better, how was that a real gain? We need to look critically, moreover, at the many ways in which women maintained themselves. Their strategies were not always positive, and so a most difficult question has to be asked: What have the victims wrought?

It is interesting to see, if we can, whether women maintained themselves either better than or—perhaps more accurately—differently from men. However, the discovery of difference is often pernicious because it helps us to forget the context of these supposed strengths—oppression—and to ignore the possibility that they may be only apparent. To suggest that among those Jews who lived through the Holocaust, women survived better than men is to move toward acceptance or valorization of oppression. Oppression does not make people better; oppression makes people oppressed. There is no sense in fighting or even understanding oppression if we maintain that the values and practices of the oppressed are not only better than those of the oppressor but in some objective sense "a model for humanity and the new society," as Barbara Burris wrote in an essay published in 1973 in a volume entitled *Radical Feminism*, edited by Anne Koedt. This is not to say that there are no differences between men and women in values or ways of relating to institutions. It *is* to question our interpretations of the conceptual and political import of such differences.

My attempt, then, to emphasize friendships among women in the camps gives a false or misleading impression that oppression is only external and not internal as well. Why the silence about the internalized oppression of the Jewish women survivors? To avoid another dimension of the horror of the Holocaust or of oppression in general? In my early work I seemed to be saying that in spite of rape, abuse, and the murder of babies, in spite of starvation, separations, losses, terror, and violence, in spite of everything ugly and disgusting, women bonded, loved each other. Must we not ask how many women, at what cost, for how long, under what conditions?

These were among the questions I raised in my self-critique at the Berkshire conference. I said that my focus on friendship, affection, and so on distorted the understanding of the larger situation in which those experiences may have played only a small role. Talk of friendship allowed those of us who heard the women's stories to admire them. Though it helped to muffle the terrible surrounding sounds of the Holocaust and even to give some peace and comfort, this woman-centered perspective and the questions it addressed were misguided.

I went on to say that the work was not useless even if the perspectives and questions were wrong. I thought we needed some new questions. What does oppression do to us? Is women's culture liberating? How can it be if it was nourished in oppression? Does suffering make us better people? Does the apparent need for gender pride get in the way of the truth? Do people lie in order survive, no matter what the level of oppression? Are the stories survivors tell us less about the Holocaust than about their present suffering and their attempts to survive the memory of the past? Do women survivors transform the story of the Holocaust and their relations with other women in order to live with themselves? Why do many women survivors believe they survived better than men? Does that have to do with the reality of the Holocaust or with women's return to traditional roles and expectations afterwards? Were women's friendships in the camps really as crucial, in a positive sense, as many who were interviewed claimed? Is there more to the story than the women are likely to report no matter what questions are posed? Why is it important for us to believe that these friendships or relationships were so central to their stories? What is at stake for us? What is resistance? Is anything an oppressed woman does an act of resistance? Do descriptions of the lack of active or armed resistance against the enemy, whether by Jews (men or women) or others (e.g., Russian prisoners of war, Roma, homosexual men or lesbian women) have to lead us to defend the inaction and even glorify it? The oft-heard phrase "survival is resistance" is a mystification in response to which at least one further question can be posed: What do we say about the dead? And for myself, how can I be true to the material given me by those I interviewed while raising such a question? What are the political effects or consequences of studying women and the Holocaust?

In closing I said, "These questions and the critique out of which they come not only have enabled me to see where I have been but also show me in what direction I need to move." There was a big crowd at this talk and the subsequent panel discussion. Some were really angry at what I had said. Some were very upset at what they considered my stridency in giving this paper. I know I was emotional about it, but I suspect the tone was easy to hear as strident, and perhaps it was. Some people also thought that I was blaming others for my failings rather than taking responsibility for them.

In 1989 I took a job with the US Holocaust Memorial Museum as special assistant to the museum director on academic matters. In 1991 I became research director for the Permanent Exhibition. Life at USHMM became particularly intense in 1993, when my new position as director of oral history and the opening of the museum took me away from my research, but I continued working on a book on women and the Holocaust. I had an agent in New York, Candida Donadio, who tried to sell the book and received somewhere in the neighborhood of fifteen rejections. The sole interested editor was Elizabeth Sifton at Pantheon, which disbanded just as I was to talk with her. When she tried again in her new job at Knopf, she was told that they had too many books on the Holocaust.

I was more than disappointed. I began to believe that I should stop trying to get the book published. Although I continued to write some as well as give lectures on the topic of women and the Holocaust, I worried that I had nothing more to say. I was not a historian, and I felt it was up to the historians, political scientists, sociologists, literary analysts, and others to pursue this work. I felt I'd opened up a field of research but couldn't do more than I'd already done, perhaps because the only language I knew was English, which meant I had no direct access to original sources. I consulted all the books I could find in English for figures that might suggest differences between men and women who were deported to ghettos and camps, Jewish men and women in particular, but the figures I found were often discrepant, which was a big problem when I was trying to say something clear on the subject. Moreover, the research itself was often extremely tedious, hard, and depressing. Still, I kept thinking about the issue throughout the 1990s and published a paper about it, "Genocide and Gender: A Split Memory," in *Gender and Catastrophe*, a 1997 volume edited by Ronit Lentin. In what follows I summarize what I wrote in that paper.

The impulse to neutralize the issue of sex by treating it as nonexistent or insignificant is entirely understandable. The possible rape of mothers, grandmothers, sisters, friends, or lovers during the Holocaust is difficult to face. The possibility that mothers or sisters or lovers "voluntarily" used sex to procure food or protection is equally difficult to absorb, if not more so. Experiences connected with sex, whether negative or positive, are understandably troublesome, but if we dismiss situations that relate so specifically to women, it is well-nigh impossible to understand the victimization of women and really see Jewish women as victims.

Irene Eber, a survivor and a scholar of Chinese intellectual history and literature, once told me, "Male memory can confront women as victims, but cannot confront male oppression. . . . The same may be true for women survivors. They can see themselves as Nazi victims but not as victims of Jewish men or even Nazi men." It has been difficult to confront the fact that Jewish women were victims as Jewish women, not only because Jewish men exploited them, but also because Jewish men could not protect their women and children from the Nazis. "It has clearly been too difficult to contemplate the extent to which gender counted in the exploitation and murder of Jewish women," I wrote in conclusion, "and the extent to which the sexism of Nazi ideology and the sexism of the Jewish community met in a tragic and involuntary alliance."

My last paper on the subject, "The Split Between Gender and the Holocaust," was published in *Women in the Holocaust* (1998), edited by Dalia Ofer and Lenore J. Weitzman. An excerpt follows.

> The Holocaust is defined by death. In this domain of death, it is crude if not obscene to avoid talking about gender. . . . To the Nazis, Jewish women were not simply Jews; they were Jewish women, and they were treated accordingly in the system of annihilation. Research suggests that more Jewish women were deported than Jewish men, and more women than men were selected for death in the extermination camps. Jewish men did not stand in line for women when it came to the killing operations. Jewish women stood in their own lines and were killed as Jewish women. Nor can Jewish men stand in for Jewish women as we try to understand their everyday life during the Holocaust, with its terror, loss, escape, hope, humor, friendships, love, work, starvation, beatings, rape, abortions, and killings. Jewish women and men experienced unrelieved suffering during the Holocaust. Jewish women carried the burdens of sexual victimization, pregnancy, abortion, childbirth, killing of newborn babies in the camps to save the mothers, care of children, and separation from children. For Jewish women the Holocaust produced a set of experiences, responses, and memories that do not always parallel those of Jewish men. As one survivor said, "Everything else is the same. But there are certain things that are different." If in the gas chambers or before the firing squads all Jews seemed alike to the Nazis, the path to this end was not always the same for women and men.

The end—namely, annihilation or death—does not describe or explain the process.

When I first began speaking and writing about women and the Holocaust, criticism came quickly. Many thought that I was violating a sacred event by raising questions about it that had not been raised before, desecrating the meaning of the Holocaust simply by asking about women and their particular experiences.

I once gave a lecture in a Connecticut synagogue and quoted Hannah Arendt. An older man stood up and berated me. "She slept with a Nazi, so what right have you to quote such a person in your paper?" He was referring to Arendt's brief affair with her teacher Martin Heidegger in the 1920s. I was surprised at the blunt question and taken aback by its stupidity. I could feel my anger rising. I said something to the effect that she slept with him before the Nazis took over and that he was not a Nazi at the time. The man yelled something about Heidegger firing his teacher and colleague Edmund Husserl at Freiburg University, and I retorted that Hannah Arendt had left Germany by the time Heidegger became rector at Freiburg and that she had criticized him for taking the position. I said I wasn't happy that she'd had an affair with him but that she was so right about so much that I had to use her. I pointed out that she'd been arrested by the Gestapo in 1933 and then released, whereupon she fled Germany and ended up in Paris, where she worked for several years with Zionist organizations seeking to relocate Jewish youth to Palestine. In May 1940, by order of the military governor of Paris, she was sent to the Gurs internment camp, from which she managed to escape later that year. I said all that to this man with rising anger, and perhaps I went too far, but I was overwrought. A great deal of emotional baggage of one sort or another always seemed to accompany any discussion of women and the Holocaust.

He was not the first person to yell at me or the last. Some people were upset because they thought I was dividing Jewish men from

Jewish women in such a way that the significance of Jewishness in the Holocaust would be lost, or if not lost, obscured by a huge controversy amongst contemporary Jews. No such issue arose in discussions of the Jewish councils or the Jewish police in the ghettos or the actions of particular individuals (e.g., Chaim Rumkowski, head of the Jewish Council of Elders in the Lodz ghetto, or Adam Czerniakov, Nazi-installed mayor of the Warsaw ghetto), but a discussion of women was somehow going to destroy the meaning of the Holocaust. This was difficult to hear, and I heard it over and over again. Sometimes there was support for what I was saying and a debate would occur in an audience, but overall it was difficult to continue speaking and writing about women and the Holocaust because the response could be so hostile.

When I started at the Holocaust Memorial Museum, I suggested that it was important to include women in our exhibition. The museum did have what was called "The Women's Room," and I was instrumental in getting it removed because I thought women's experiences should be part of the entire exhibition and not ghettoized into a single room. However, getting rid of it did not result in much of a change; there was very little about women's experiences in other parts of the museum's exhibition. I could not find a sympathetic ear on this issue among those who mattered in the museum administration, although it is perhaps telling that I did help to secure exhibition space on gays and Roma.

When I was asked to be the museum's director of education, I had one requirement: I wanted to remain director of oral history. I also wanted my work on women and the Holocaust to be made public in the announcement of my new position. In the first draft of the announcement, this work was not mentioned. I protested to Sara Bloomfield, the museum's director, and she decided to include my publications on women and the Holocaust, even though she thought it would be problematic. I may well have said that if she didn't include this information, I wouldn't take the position, but I'm not sure. In any case, I should have realized that my role in opening the field of women and the Holocaust for research was going to cause trouble at the museum.

In May 1998, the political commentator Gabriel Schoenfeld wrote an op-ed piece for the *Wall Street Journal*, "The 'Cutting Edge' of Holocaust Studies," followed in June by an essay in *Commentary*, "Auschwitz and the Professors." In both pieces he attacked "the academization" of the Holocaust into various fields of study as attempts to reduce "the fathomless evil of the Holocaust in the detached, dispassionate environment of a university lecture hall." And in both pieces he attacked me and other feminist scholars, claiming that our work was trivializing the Holocaust.

These pieces caused a firestorm at the museum. Not only did Schoenfeld say that any feminist working on women and the Holocaust was doing something despicable because the work was serving "the purpose of consciousness-raising—i.e., propaganda"; he also implied that I was the worst of feminists for perhaps the worst of reasons, career advancement, and that the museum should never have appointed me director of education.

In a letter to the editor of the *Wall Street Journal*, published on May 26, 1998, I wrote that Schoenfeld's op-ed piece "distorts my words, takes quotes out of context, and puts them into interpretations which bear no relationship to my ideas. . . . To imply that I 'assign co-responsibility for the catastrophe [of the Holocaust]' to Jewish men and Nazis is a claim so vile as to not warrant a reply. No one who has conscientiously read my work or heard me speak could come up with such an outrageous conclusion." I went on to note that "Holocaust scholarship has evolved to take into account the different experiences of children and adults, rich and poor, religious and secular, as well as women and men. Together with age and class, sex and gender are universal categories— being in one category or another always has consequences."

The museum administration was rattled. They claimed they had no idea I had written the articles Schoenfeld cited. Of course I'd included these articles and other work in the material I submitted to the museum in my application for the director of education position, and if they hadn't read the material, that was their problem. Although they seemed pleased with my *Wall Street Journal* letter in defense of my work, they did not support me. Apparently they were frightened of Schoenfeld and the people who might agree with him. Although it took them about fifteen months to remove me as director of education, they finally succeeded, and I returned to my position as director of oral history. A good friend of mine, Judy Goldstein (founding director of Humanity in Action, whose students I led in discussion of the museum's Permanent Exhibition for many years), later saw Schoenfeld at a party, and he told her how happy he was that he'd played a pivotal role in removing me as director of education.

If you visit the museum today, you will find that the Permanent Exhibition has not changed since the opening. The museum staff is now in the process of thinking through potential changes, though I have no idea whether those concerned with the changes are also thinking about including material specific to gender and/or women and the Holocaust.

Dr. Lisa Leff, director of the Jack, Joseph and Morton Mandel Center for Advanced Holocaust Studies, formerly the Research Institute of the USHMM, wrote to me during the 2020 coronavirus pandemic and cited a number of examples on the topic of women and the Holocaust at the museum. There are two primary source collections: ITS Primary Source Supplement (https://archive.org/details/bib259530_001_001) and Experiencing History: Primary Source Collection on Gender, Sexuality and the Holocaust (https://perspectives.ushmm.org/collection/gender-sexuality-and-the-holocaust). There have been a number of seminars and workshops for museum faculty: in 2017, the Hess Faculty Seminar on Gender and Sexuality in the Holocaust; in 2012, the Silberman Faculty Seminar on Teaching the Gendered History of the Holocaust; and in 2004, a Research Workshop on Gender and the Holocaust.

There have also been a number of fellows doing research on gender, among them Marta Havryshko, the 2019-2020 Diane and Howard Wohl Fellow (https://www.ushmm.org/research/about-the-mandel-center/all-fellows-and-scholars/dr-marta-havryshko), whose project was "Sexual Violence Against Jewish Women in Nazi-Occupied Ukraine." A former fellow, Anna Hájková, is the author of *The Last Ghetto: An Everyday History of Theresienstadt* (Oxford University Press, 2020), which raises questions about gender. Sara Horowitz was a senior fellow in 2009, and the title of her project was "Gender, Genocide, and Jewish Memory: Culture, Memory and the Holocaust" (https://www.ushmm.org/research/about-the-mandel-center/all-fellows-and-scholars/sara-horowitz-2009). What isn't apparent simply in the list of fellows' topics, and what Dr. Leff found striking and revealing, were the discussions that took place at the weekly meetings of fellows. Everyone, she told me, was asked questions about "gender or women, and has looked into the different experiences of men and women.... a fellow's topic which seems generic—for example a current fellow working on refugees in Shanghai, or another working on the Kovno ghetto—often will have a gender or women's history dimension to it.... we have all learned that women's history is not just 'add women and stir'—it gives a really different view of what happened when we take women's experiences into account." If gender was a difficult topic in the Research Institute when I was at the museum, it no longer seems so in the Mandel Center.

Online, at www.ushmm.org, the Women During the Holocaust entry in the Holocaust Encyclopedia contains statements taking note of "brutal persecution that was sometimes unique to the gender of the victims. ... During deportation operations, pregnant women and mothers of small children were consistently labeled 'incapable of work.' They were sent to killing centers, where camp officials often included them in the first groups to be sent to the gas chambers." There are other significant statements of this sort in this and other entries about women. Still, there is no mention of studies about how gender operated against victims and how gender operated for perpetrators. Further, there is no mention about how relations (including sexual ones) operated between victims or between perpetrators and victims. While the museum hierarchy may not feel as threatened as they did when Schoenfeld's articles came out in the late nineties, there is no reason to think that gender has become a central topic for the museum as a whole.

A Public Program on Gender and Genocide was to take place at the museum on March 19, 2020, but it was canceled because of the coronavirus. The announcement for the program stated:

> Until recently, gender was ignored in genocide studies. Women who were victims and survivors of the Holocaust were considered to have had the "same experience" as men.
>
> Today we know better. History shows that gender is weaponized in war. . . . Through conflict-era memoirs and survivor testimonies, we are learning women's unique experiences during the Holocaust, in the Rwanda and Bosnia genocides of the 1990s, and today, in Iraq, Syria, and Burma.

This sounds as if a change has come to another part of the museum, but two of the three speakers listed in the announcement, although well-versed in other genocides, were not experts in Holocaust history: Sareta Ashraph, senior legal adviser to the Simon-Skjodt Center for the Prevention of Genocide; and Sara Darehshori, principal of the investigative firm Vestry Laight, and former prosecutor at the International Criminal Tribunal of Rwanda. The third speaker was to be Helen Epstein, who is a journalist, author, and editor of *Franci's War: A Woman's Story of Survival*, her mother's memoir of surviving World War II in Terezin and other concentration camps. While I have great respect for all her work and am in no way criticizing her, my point here is that she is not a scholar of women in the Holocaust, nor is she known for any scholarly contribution to the field. Consequently, while I am pleased to note this planned program at the museum, I am not sure whether the museum is ready or willing to understand the specific importance of the work of scholars of women and the Holocaust and feature them in a public setting. There are any number of such scholars to choose from, to name just a few: Anna Hájková, Atina Grossman, Marion Kaplan, Judith Tydor Baumel-Schwartz, Dalia Ofer, Wendy Lower, Marta Havryshko, Na'ama Shik, Dorota Glowacka, Janet Jacobs, and Sara R. Horowitz.

In closing, I am proud that I contributed to opening up the field of women and the Holocaust. I am also proud to have been on the founding staff of the US Holocaust Memorial Museum. The apparent conflict between my work at the museum and my research on women is something I have come to accept, even if reluctantly. I always seemed to be in conflict with the institutions that employed me, but the battle over women's experiences during the Holocaust was one worth fighting. It was the trajectory I chose. As I said at the outset, the Holocaust shaped my life.

FOUR

Oral History

The strands are all there: to the memory nothing is ever lost.
—Eudora Welty, *One Writer's Beginning*

"I have done that," says my memory, "I cannot have done that," says my pride, and remains inexorable. Eventually—memory yields.
—Friedrich Nietzsche, *Beyond Good and Evil*

In 1992, when I had been working for several years as research director for the Permanent Exhibition at the US Holocaust Memorial Museum, the position of director of oral history opened up in advance of the official opening of the museum, scheduled for April 22, 1993. I was reluctant to apply, possibly because I had elevated ideas about what was an appropriate job for me as a PhD in philosophy. In the end I decided to try for the job, with the encouragement of my colleagues at the museum, only to discover that the deadline for applications had passed. The head of Human Resources suggested that I write a short note to the museum's director and deputy director to ask for permission to apply belatedly. On the same day that he received this note, the director, Shaike Weinberg, returned it with the message "Please apply."

It seemed clear from this that Shaike wanted me to have the position, but he invited me to lunch to discuss some concerns he had. I had been angry at how the museum was being run, and at staff meetings I had asked questions and made critical statements. For example, I remember being very angry about the firing of a staff member. While many other staff members signed a petition against the firing, no one at our meetings said a word about the petition. I thought it was important to raise the issue, and I did so at a meeting led by the director and the deputy director. My comments on this and other issues were often greeted with applause from the staff, whereupon Shaike and his deputy director would simply leave. They never took on any criticisms from me or anyone else.

At our lunch, Shaike expressed concern that I would continue to make such public criticisms as director of oral history. He suggested that it pleased me to speak out this way, like some 1960s rebel. I said that it didn't, that I was just frustrated because I couldn't change museum practices that I found so problematic. He went on to say that he wanted me to stop embarrassing the leadership in public settings. I admitted that I was naïve and had no idea how to change things except by talking as I did. I promised that I would never embarrass the leadership publicly again; if I had issues or disagreements, I would come and talk with him or others privately. I kept my promise.

In retrospect, I suspect that I was secretly complimented by Shaike's picture of me as a rebel. He was probably right that my outspokenness in front of my colleagues pleased me. I knew I was gratified that the staff thought well of me, but I also knew that in the end what I was doing was ineffective. I was and remain grateful to Shaike for his honesty and directness. I said that I wished we had talked earlier, and he agreed.

At that point we probably hadn't spoken for about a year, so we'd both missed out on what could have been a fruitful relationship.

After this lunch, it was clear that I would get the job, and I soon received the appointment letter. Whatever thoughts I may have had about the inadequacy of the position vanished rapidly. Now I had to learn how to manage, something I'd never done before. In addition, I would have to interview survivors, a prospect that alarmed me. Before I came to the museum, I had started a Women and the Holocaust project and had completed some fifteen audio interviews with women survivors, but I never thought they were very good, so I was worried about doing video interviews for the museum. The stakes seemed much higher now that I'd be doing interviews for an established Holocaust institution.

I called Sandy Bradley, a filmmaker and interviewer who worked for the museum on Permanent Exhibition films and had done interviews for the Smithsonian, and asked for her advice. She gave me two suggestions. First, an interviewer should listen more than talk—in other words, learn to be silent and be alert for the unexpected, learn when to ask a question and when to refrain. Second, the interview is not the place to exhibit your ego and your smartness, not the place to demonstrate that you know more than the interviewee, even if you think you know more or you actually do.

I also asked Sandy why people responded to her so well even when she asked what could be considered stupid or ill-conceived questions. She suggested that while questions were very important, the interaction itself created a relationship that even "stupid" or "ill-conceived" questions could not destroy, and I used her ideas when I later wrote the introduction to the USHMM *Oral History Interview Guidelines*. I never forgot her advice, although I was only sometimes able to follow it.

My first interview for the museum, on January 28, 1993, was with Bill Lowenberg, a survivor and the vice-president of the USHMM Council.

I was incredibly nervous because I wasn't sure I could carry it off and I knew it would be publicly available. (It can be found at the museum and on the museum's website, along with all the other interviews I conducted as director of oral history.) Bill spoke of being in a hypnotic cocoon that he did not want to leave. Since his life was good, he asked, "Why should I open up too much?" He characterized our interview as a travelogue with "none of the gory stuff." Apparently, I wanted survivors to go beyond what was easy or familiar, beyond the story they told everyone. What Bill said was both important and disappointing to me. His agreement to do an interview did not necessarily mean that what was beneath the surface would be revealed.

As nervous as I'd been about the interview, I wrote afterward that I felt comfortable and loved the puzzle of the process, that it felt right and it seemed I might become a really good interviewer. I had my comeuppance when I heard from Shaike, who had watched the interview and told me that I had talked too much. I was surprised because I hadn't remembered the interview that way, but when I watched the video myself, I was shocked. It was obvious that I often asked my questions too quickly without waiting for Bill to move into other areas on his own, though it's also true that had I not asked some of these questions, there were some answers I would not have heard. For example, at the very beginning of the interview, Bill quickly spoke about his family going from Germany to Holland at the end of 1936. I interrupted and asked him to slow down. "Let's not go there yet," I said.

> Bill: Okay.
>
> Joan: Let's get back a little bit. You were very young when the Nazis took over in 1933?
>
> Bill: Yah, I was six years old.
>
> Joan: Yes, do you remember any particular change in your life in terms of friends and school?
>
> Bill: Indeed. I lived on a street, I remember vividly . . .

He then went on to speak about how differently he was treated in school because he was Jewish: he had to sit in the back of the room, the other children would not play with him, etc. He recounted other indignities that showed how he experienced anti-Semitism as a child. Still, in spite of my good questions, I noticed how often I interrupted his train of thought.

After watching the interview, I went to Shaike and told him that I realized it wasn't good. He demurred: "I never said it wasn't a good interview, I only said that you talked too much." Of course I had turned his criticism of parts of the interview into a negation of the entire interview, which was not atypical of my response to criticism.

Eventually, I was able to get over this negativity and think about preparing for my second interview, with Charlene Perlmutter Schiff, a Polish survivor who escaped from the ghetto in Horochow, her birthplace, in 1942, along with her mother. I was now more than convinced that silence on the part of the interviewer was crucial. Before the official interview, I went to Charlene's home in Virginia and spent an afternoon with her. At the time I thought I should do this kind of pre-interview routinely, as a way of trying to establish an intimate relationship with the interviewee in advance, but this proved impossible both financially and practically.

During that conversation at her home, Charlene told me haltingly that she had drunk her own urine while hiding in the forests near Horochow and was ashamed to say anything about it. When she arrived for the actual interview, on March 23, 1993, I suggested that it might be important to talk about this so people could understand something of the terrible difficulties she faced, especially since she was only thirteen at the time. I had thought about this a great deal, and I promised not to raise the matter unless she volunteered it. And she did, without my asking her anything directly.

How I lived in the forest, or in the forests, I don't know, but it's an amazing thing, when one is hungry and completely demoralized, you become inventive. I never, even when I say it I don't believe it, I ate worms, I ate bugs, . . . I ate anything that I could put in my mouth, and I don't know, sometimes I would get very ill, there were some wild mushrooms, I'm sure they were poison, I don't know, poisonous ones, I was ill, my stomach was a mess, but I still put it in my mouth because I needed to have something to chew. I drank water from puddles, snow, anything that I can get hold of. Sometimes I would sneak into potato cellars the farmers have around their villages and that was a good hiding place because it was a little warmer in the winter, but there were rodents there and all. And, to say that I ate raw rats, yes, I did. Apparently, I wanted to live very, very badly, because I did indescribable things. I ate things that no one would dream of being able to. Somehow I survived. I don't know why, I keep asking myself, but I did. To this day, I'm still looking for my parents and my sister, none of them survived. I tried to go back, and it seems every year I remember more details, but I try not to, I try to forget, but I can't. I feel that I'm a prisoner of my memories, and I'm imprisoned in a jail that I can't break away from. But, I do feel that I have a mandate, and I must speak out for the millions who never had a chance. I'm their spokesperson. I have to tell the world what went on, so we can learn from these past mistakes, from the cruelty, and from the inhumanity of man towards man. . . . I don't know how I can tell you much more, except to tell you that I lived just like an animal. I ate and drank human waste, but I never killed another human being, and I don't think that should I meet face to face with people who are responsible for my parents' and my sister's murder, and for the millions of others, I don't think I'm capable of killing another human being. I could even forgive, but I cannot forget, and I do not want the world to forget.

There is a real question here about the ethics of asking survivors to talk about matters that may be deeply uncomfortable or compromising or humiliating. Should an interviewer ask such questions? I think so, and yet I wonder. It seems crucial for the historical record, but is it crucial in terms of the well-being of the survivor, and should an interviewer be concerned?

Recently, I asked a colleague and friend, Sarah Ogilvie, who had assisted the Romanian historian Radu Ioanid in choosing photographs for the Permanent Exhibition, whether she and Radu ever discussed the photos, which were so often difficult to look at. Her answer surprised me. She told me that they did not discuss the photos—usually horrific—once their work was done. When they put the photos aside, they talked about their lives. They divided their private selves from their professional selves and had no discussions about the effect these photos had on their lives. This made me think more about how I and other interviewers wanted survivors to reveal their experiences, no matter how horrendous or difficult. Would those we interviewed divide their lives in a similar fashion?

When Charlene talked about hiding in the forest, she mentioned singing to herself. I asked if she remembered what she sang. She said yes, she remembered several songs, "but I'm not a singer, really," and then she tried to sing a lullaby that her mother had sung to her. She started, stopped, and cried some. I said nothing, just looked at her, desperately trying to maintain my silence. She started again, got a little further, and stopped. Again I said nothing. I did not offer sympathetic words, did not attempt to soothe her or tell her she needn't go on, as I was tempted to do. I just looked at her. In the end, she sang the whole song with tears streaming down her face, as reflected in the transcript, though without the tears or her inflections or her expressions or any of the other human responses that a transcript can't reveal.

Lulej, Lulej—

I'm sorry, I can't.

Lulej, Lulej,Lulej ma malinka ...

Lulej, lulej, siwy oczka z mrug

Nadwszystkimi, na dobry dzieczmy, Czuwa, Czuwa, Czuwa

"It means go to sleep, my little one," Charlene explained, "close your eyes, and all good children—over all good children watches an angel. I feel her presence now. I have so many questions. . . . I have no answers, and it bothers me, and I don't know how I can die in peace because all these questions will be unanswered." I am convinced that had I interrupted and told Charlene that she didn't have to continue, I would not have heard the song.

Toward the end of the interview, Charlene and I had the following exchange, prompted by my asking about her penknife.

Q: How did use your penknife?

A: Oh, the penknife was used for a million and one—for everything. I used it to help me dig my little holes in the forest. I used it to cut up my potatoes, my raw potatoes, to cut vegetables from the gardens, or I sometimes would get these wild nuts in the forest, and in order to open them I would use the penknife because I didn't have anything else. I started doing it with my teeth, but my teeth were hurting badly. I don't think I could have survived without my penknife.

Q: Is that how you killed the rats?

A: Yes.

Q: This is difficult to express, isn't it?

A: Yes, it's difficult for me today to believe that I stooped that low, that I did that, but I did. I'm not proud of it. I feel very humiliated to share this with you, but, yes, I did it.

Q: Well, I'm grateful that you told me.

A: Thank you.

Q: I know this sounds like a silly question, because you used the word humiliation, you were put in such a horrible situation—

A: I never shared these kind of details. When I speak at schools and all, I'm very—not superficial, but I don't go into such details, because I don't feel comfortable talking about it, and I do feel humiliated, but I guess it has to be told and I hope whoever listens will respect me regardless. I did that to survive. And, perhaps, part of my survival, the meaning of my survival, is to talk about it now so people will know. Again, I feel that my parents have given me such a solid early childhood that I did have the strength to survive and to end up now reasonably well.

It was clear to me as I looked at Charlene that she had left our interview space and gone back in time. Is the information about her penknife important? For understanding the Holocaust, perhaps not. It is a small detail. But it does tell us something more about what Charlene says she did and saw. I continued the interview by asking her what she felt.

Q: Were you feeling fear all the time?

A: Yes, yes. I still feel it when I talk about it, I still feel fear. And, I don't know, it's also a very—it's an indescribable kind of feeling, because fear is something that you fear people, you fear, you know, emotions, you fear nature, I was fearing fear itself. I was always in fear for everything that was going on. I was always—I was not at ease with anything that was going on in my life. But, while we were still in the ghetto, while my mother was still there, she was such a—she was solid as a rock, and she gave us all the comfort that we needed, and that was enough.

Q: So, you never saw her cry?

A: Never saw her cry, never, not when they took my father away, no. She just hugged us. She took my sister and me close to her and she hugged us. We cried, she did not. She probably cried that night, but she didn't cry then, no. She took his jacket to the ghetto with us, the jacket—the sports jacket that he was going to put on, because he was always a very formal dresser, you know, and she took it. She had it in the river with her, yes.

Q: She was wearing it?

A: Yes.

Q: So, they were very close.

A: Yes, they were very close. They were very close, from what I saw they were very loving, very understanding of one another, and complimenting one another on everything they did and everything they said. And, I mean, I was telling this to some of my friends and they said, ah, I mean, you are idealizing it, there's no such a human being to be so—I mean, two human beings to be so perfect and all. I said, "My parents and my sister were perfect," and that's the way I remember them. I don't remember one flaw, nothing. I can't remember anything that they did that I didn't admire, and I was very, very lucky, very lucky.

After my interview with Charlene, I jotted down some notes: "I thought a good deal about how to be quiet, how to force myself to wait beyond my patience level. I remember waiting and waiting even though I really wanted to ask a question. I noticed that Charlene often went on to talk about what I was going to ask." It was then that I realized that waiting and being silent allowed an interviewee to talk at his or her own pace and to reveal what an interviewer might ask about anyway, so that a direct question might well be an intrusion.

I remembered Sandy Bradley's suggestions for interviewers. Her first piece of advice, about listening, was now entirely clear to me. I learned that listening was a most difficult task, whether in interviewing a stranger (a survivor of the Holocaust or of another tragedy, or someone who is going to speak about his or her life, whether of historical significance or simply of human significance), or in talking with a friend or lover, or in teaching a class, or in doing therapy with a patient. In any kind of interview, you must focus on what someone says, not on what you expected them to say, what you hoped they would say, or what you thought they should say. Listening in an interview demands a high level of concentration because listening demands silence and we find it difficult to be silent when people talk. Often we are afraid of silence. We go over things in our heads, prepare what we want to say instead of listening. I have a tendency to interrupt people when I think I know what they're going to say, sometimes because I have something I need to say myself, so trying not to do this during an interview, let alone in my personal life, was complicated for me. Eventually, I was able to be more silent and controlled in my responses during an interview, though I suspect less so in my personal life.

When it came to Sandy's second piece of advice, I had no need to demonstrate that I knew more than the interviewees did. I wanted them to speak in as much detail as possible. I didn't need to show them what I knew, and I also understood that what I knew came from books, whereas what survivors knew came from experience. It was their experience in all its concreteness that I wanted, so even if they offered a "mistaken" story, it was still their story, and therein lay its significance. I might know more than they did about historical events that they hadn't experienced, but I could never know more about what they lived through.

I ended up with what I thought was a simple technique. Early on, I had some idea of a particular survivor's story line from the pre-interview. I put that story onto note cards and tried to remember it so I wouldn't have to look at my cards, which I thought might be distracting for the interviewee. I began in somewhat the same way each time: How nice to see you. Where were you born and when? Tell me about your parents and siblings—that kind of thing. I had a few arranged questions based on the pre-interview, but I never felt comfortable putting down questions beforehand. Mostly my questions came to me as the interviewee spoke, in the moment, with the person sitting in front of me. Some of the interviewers I hired had written questions they were prepared to ask all through the interview, which didn't mean that they didn't respond well to the unexpected, just that their technique was different from mine.

I never thought that there was only one way to do interviews, even if I had some criticisms of other techniques, such as those of the Shoah Foundation and a long-term project at Yale. I was not sure that Yale's practice of having two interviewers for every interviewee—one a therapist and the other a scholar of Holocaust history and/or literature—was a good idea. I thought that two interviewers were a distraction for the interviewee, and perhaps something of a distraction for the interviewers. As for the Shoah Foundation, they had decided that Jewish survivors would not want to talk with gentile interviewers. Given our experience at the museum with Sandy Bradley, I found that conclusion terribly narrow and mistaken. I now wonder about all my criticisms. I wonder whether interviewers who had prearranged questions went further than I did, but I never asked any of them about this part of their technique, which seems strange to me. I believed then and still believe that different styles of interviewing are acceptable and that there is no one correct interview technique, yet my criticisms seemed to belie this position or to suggest that there were limits to my belief.

The notion of different styles is as true of interviewing as it is of musical interpretation. If you listen to Horowitz, Rubinstein, Argerich, Guller, Wang, Pollini, Trifonov, Lang, Levit, or any number of others playing a Beethoven sonata, will you be hearing the same piece of music? Yes. But will it sound different? Yes. Is one style right and the other wrong? No. The issue of taste is a separate matter from right and wrong.

Interviewing is primarily an art, which means that successful strategies will vary. The same person may give different and even divergent interviews to different people, depending on the interviewer or the day and whether it's a sad or happy day. But that doesn't mean that there are no limits or boundaries. For example, as I mentioned earlier, interviewees should not be argued with. They may make mistakes, but it is not the interviewer's role to correct them. They may say things that might stimulate conversation, but interviewers don't converse, we listen. Still, carefully placed questions can indicate without confrontation that there are problems in the testimony. When someone says that Dr. Mengele selected them at Auschwitz, the interviewer might ask, "How did you find out it was Mengele who selected you?" The answer usually reveals something that may be helpful to a researcher.

Josef Mengele was one of twenty or more doctors at Auschwitz who selected people to live or die. He is probably best remembered for his experiments on twins. His notoriety is such that most survivors of Auschwitz-Birkenau claim that they were selected by him when they arrived at the camp. Even if they arrived before he was there, they identify Mengele as having been at the ramp choosing them to enter the camp and their relatives to be killed. The number of survivors who mention his name is so large that one can only assume that "Mengele" has become a kind of public symbol or public substitute for all the doctors of Auschwitz at the selection ramp. As Helen Zippy Tichauer née Spitzer told me in one of our conversations over the years, "If Mengele had actually been at the ramp as much as survivors claim, he would still be there." She was one of the few survivors who actually had contact with Mengele.

Another example of problematic testimony has to do with the prevalent view that women didn't menstruate in Auschwitz because some chemical was put in the food. This claim is made regularly in spite of the fact that those who repeat it have no direct knowledge of kitchen procedures in Auschwitz, nor do they have evidence of any kind, only rumor. If an interviewer asks, "How did you find this out?" anyone who listens carefully to the response can determine whether there is a problem with the interviewee's perspective. Eventually, this claim about a chemical in the food became part of many survivors' stories. Further, while it is true that women didn't menstruate in Auschwitz, there is significant forgetfulness about or inattention to the fact that women also stopped menstruating in the ghettos. For some reason, the camp story has taken hold, so an interviewee is rarely asked about the issue of menstruation in the ghettos.

Because much of the content of the interviews I did was tragic and terrifying, learning to listen also meant that I had to be able to hear my own fears. I think this is true generally, because all sorts of interviewees tell stories that may have difficult content for any interviewer. There is no doubt that I often wanted to protect myself from what interviewees had to say, but I had to try to learn to listen to everything about which the interviewee was able to speak. This was not always possible. Sometimes I was shy and afraid to ask more. Sometimes I was scared, even when I didn't know it. I had to be able to ask about anything in a way that invited rather than repelled a response. This meant that difficult questions had to be posed in a simple, straightforward way, in a tone that was neutral or sympathetic, never judgmental. I learned that if I exposed my fears by asking a question emotionally, interviewees would often respond by attempting to protect me rather than answering the question. While interviewers must respect the interviewee's limits, we also must try not to allow our own limitations to curtail the stories that interviewees can tell us. It is crucial to learn what it is we are afraid of as interviewers so that our wish to hide and to protect ourselves, a wish common to most people, does not interfere with the interview.

An example worth repeating comes from the first interview I did for my project on women and the Holocaust, in 1979. (Actually, it was the first interview I had ever done.) The interviewee was Susan Cernyak-Spatz, who was initially sent to the Theresienstadt labor-deportation camp and then to Auschwitz-Birkenau. Susan talked about the uses of sex in Theresienstadt, where "you survived as a woman through the [Jewish] male." Of her experiences in Auschwitz-Birkenau, she spoke of an SS man's interest in her (she avoided him) and of "dating" a Pole from the men's camp at Birkenau. I did not pursue her provocative statements at the time.

In the summer of 1982, Susan revealed something new to me when I visited her at her home. She was sitting in a small room in a comfortable chair, and as I entered the room and began to sit down on the couch, she said, "I was raped in Auschwitz." I didn't say anything right away, I just looked at her. She immediately added that she wasn't gang-raped and that it was her fault anyway. I began to counsel her. I told her that this was often what rape victims said, and I tried to convince her that it wasn't her fault. Then I said, "When you are ready to speak about this, perhaps in six months, I would like to hear about it." Not surprisingly, Susan said nothing more about the rape. She knew, I suspect, that I wasn't ready or willing to hear more then.

When I came home I called my friend Gladys, a sociologist and an experienced interviewer. Gladys quickly told me what I could have asked: "What happened?" So simple and yet so far from my mind at the time. She said that an interviewer must not show judgment or fear, and must be easily and equally inquisitive about everything an interviewee says, much like a therapist. But it was not so easy to learn how to be inquisitive in a calm manner.

Although it was clear that I was a novice in the interviewing process, there was something more complicated going on. Gladys and I began to talk about the ways in which an interviewer or a researcher has fears or finds some situations too difficult to confront; over time these fears can disappear and sometimes return all over again. Our lives affect what we ask about and what we hear in interviews. But was I really afraid, or was it simply that I could not find the right question to pose? Did I lack certain crucial techniques, or did I really not want to hear? Was I befuddled by Susan's revelation because it came during a personal encounter and not an interview situation? Was I the researcher or the friend when she began to talk? I think now that all the questions apply—I was afraid, unsure, bewildered, and inexperienced.

It is one thing to figure out how to ask questions so that you can get at difficult material, still another to be able to listen. In spite of my conversation with Gladys, I didn't run to the phone to call Susan and ask Gladys's simple question. I just retained the lesson and used this story repeatedly as an example of what not to do in an interview.

A few years later, I finally decided to ask Susan what happened. She told me that she was twenty-one years old when she was deported to Auschwitz in 1943 and quickly became one of the so-called privileged prisoners. Her friends in the camp teased her about having a hole in her stomach—no matter what she ate, she was always hungry. A Polish male prisoner, tall and blond, approached her one day and offered her some sardines. She admitted to wanting to be noticed, needing attention, even affection, but said that she was not looking for sex. She suspected nothing when he told her where and when to meet him. She went. "He grabbed me and raped me." She did eat the sardines but added that she was never caught in such a situation again. Her naïveté had run out. No one knows how often this kind of thing occurred. Who asks? Who tells?

If you know what sort of information you're seeking, it appears to be a simple process to listen. Although my example is elementary, I think its simplicity reveals a good deal about how deeply we may not want to hear, and about the ways in which we avoid listening no matter how directly a survivor, male or female, may tell us what happened (for example: cannibalism, corruption, working for the Germans, hiding in a latrine, killing newborn babies, sexual violence). Sometimes we avoid because we are afraid; sometimes we avoid because we don't understand the importance of what is being said. Without a place for a particular memory, without a conceptual framework, a possibly significant piece of information will not be pursued.

As I said earlier, the same person may give different or even divergent interviews to different people, depending on the interviewer or the day. It seems that people may also give divergent statements when they are speaking about themselves and when they are writing about themselves. Only recently has it been pointed out to me by Professor Anna Hájková that in Susan's 2005 autobiography, *Protective Custody*, she gave an account of her rape very different from the one she gave me. To me she said that the rapist was Polish; in her autobiography the rapist was a "German green triangle (habitual criminal)". To me she said that he gave her sardines; in her autobiography she said he gave her "a bit of sausage." More than these differences, I think she changed the context. In her autobiography she said that the rapist "was big, blond, well-nourished, and menacing. One day he invited me to come to the store room where he would give me some food from home. Starved as I was, and not daring to contradict that brute, I went. What followed was a plain quick rape on the floor of the store room and a bit of sausage thrown at me for payment."

Susan published her autobiography in 2005. I had asked her about her rape some two decades earlier. The version of the story that rings true to me is the one she gave me then, but that's only my guess. I wish I could ask Susan about these discrepancies, but she died in 2019.

In 1984 I conducted an interview in which I seemed not to be afraid to hear. In this case the survivor, a Jewish woman who had lived in the Warsaw ghetto as a girl and was sent into hiding with Christians in Poland (let us call her Pauline), wanted to be interviewed because she knew I was working on women and the Holocaust. She knew that her story would be of interest because it illustrated the special complications that hiding from the Nazis could hold for girls or women. She wanted specifically to talk about sexual abuse, and she told me so when I called for an appointment. I didn't have to probe her about what had happened. She gave me the opening, and I gave her the opportunity, because of my research, not because I directly asked.

Pauline was eleven or twelve years old when she first went into hiding, and she told me that she had been molested by male relatives of the people who were hiding her. They threatened to denounce her if she said anything about it. She took the threats seriously: she didn't tell the young Jewish woman who checked on her periodically, she didn't tell her twin sister, and after the war she didn't tell her husband or her daughter.

"This is the first time I ever admitted this," she said during our interview, and went on to describe her experience. She told me she was physically developed for her age and was always afraid of Polish men, especially older Polish men (by which she meant any man from age twenty and up, not "old"men). On trains before travel became impossible, drunken men would rub themselves against her and expose themselves. In the family hiding her, the sons, cousins, uncles, brothers-in-law, and other older male relatives were constantly fondling her, except when the father was there, and she was always afraid she was going to be raped. "I can still smell it," she told me. "It was a tremendous fear." She was scared to say no the first time she was molested because she felt guilty and it was a complicated situation. She tried not to be alone with any of the sons, tried to see if the parents were there, if any of her girlfriends were there. "I can still feel the fear," she said. "Sometimes I think it was equally as frightening as the Germans." She added that she had nobody to complain to, that everything had to be wonderful because that's what people wanted to hear, that she was happy, everything was fine, she was alive, rescued from hell, so she had to be grateful, but "I felt guilty always."

Then she asked me a question. In respect of everything that happened, everything she and her family had suffered and seen—the humiliation in the ghetto, relatives and friends dying or taken away, the ghetto burning and people jumping out in flames—in respect of all that, was her molestation important? She really wanted to know whether gender mattered. She said that the molestation was important to her in the moment but now it was past, gone. Was this part of her story also a part of the Holocaust story? Her memory was caught between traditional versions of Holocaust history and her own personal experiences. Although she recognized her experiences as different from men's experiences, she did not know how or where to locate them in the history of the Holocaust.

It is clear to me when I compare my interviews with Susan and Pauline that while I was willing to hear what women said, I was also fearful of initiating the conversation. Many of us are afraid to ask about the intimate parts of someone's life. We stop ourselves. Perhaps this is why children of survivors may not make the best interviewers, because they may be even more afraid than others to hear about difficult matters. Fears need to be faced when they can be. Sometimes one has to try to ask about that which seems forbidden for the person even to remember, much less speak of, even if few can go there.

Interviewers can never have the same experiences as interviewees. In my case, primarily interviewing people who lived through the Holocaust—survivors of the ghettos and camps, people who went into hiding, prosecutors from the Nuremberg trials, partisans, etc.—I could be sympathetic, but I was only registering stories that remained at a remove no matter my level of empathy. One survivor, Irene Eber, told me that I had "to swim through trying to discern, develop all the sensitivities. I think especially you don't judge—you listen and try to understand."

To speak more generally, oral history is a form of autobiography with a partner, the interviewer. It is part of a genre that also includes diaries and memoirs. Testimony has more in common with memoir because it is usually produced after the events in question—a retrospective first-person account rather than a contemporary reflection on what is happening, as in a diary. When I met Charlotte Delbo, author of the trilogy *Auschwitz and After*, she told me that she wrote the first volume, *None of Us Will Return,* right after the war but kept it in a drawer for twenty years, hoping to see if it did justice to the enormity of the Holocaust. Rosette Lamont, her translator, quoted her as saying, "I wanted to make sure it would withstand the test of time, since it has to travel far into the future."

What I want from interviewees is personal reflection on their experiences and memories of these experiences. I am not looking for scholarly information from books they have read or heard about, nor am I looking for reflections based on reading or viewing documentaries or feature films about the events in question. I want details, not just the outlines of a story or general reflections on the story. I want answers to small questions about the interviewee's everyday life, whether in the ghettos or camps, in the resistance, in hiding or passing, in whatever their circumstances. I want to know what they knew, what they did and with whom, what they saw, what they thought, what they dreamt, what they feared, what they felt. In addition, I try to make room for philosophical ruminations that indicate a person's outlook on life or at least what they choose to share about it, although I must admit that these tend to be maudlin, often homilies about people's basic goodness, along with an appeal that what the Nazis did should never happen again. This sounds like a criticism, but what I mean is that most of us speak in similar terms to indicate a basic outlook and are only rarely able to talk on a philosophical level in a unique way.

Testimonies are like memoirs in that they attempt to represent the life of an individual person, though an interview is less likely to cover as much ground as a memoir. Interviews are generally more fragmentary than memoirs or diaries. An interviewer tries to elicit a picture of a person's life, but in the end it cannot be done, at least in part because there will always be a mystery about someone's life. Furthermore, when it comes to the historical events of the Holocaust, an interviewer can only get a particular view. No one experienced "the Holocaust" as such. No one person experienced the Holocaust as a whole. At best, those survivors who choose to be interviewed or to write can only speak about and for their own experiences, about their own lives: what they did, saw, heard, felt, wanted, smelled, feared, etc. And for a long while, oral historians of the Holocaust eschewed a whole range of experiences, valorizing only what happened in the camps. I originally thought that interviewing about the camps was what we should do at the Holocaust Museum, and maybe some interviews about the ghettos, but not necessarily about hiding, escaping from Germany early on, and other forms of coping or resistance. Eventually my viewpoint changed as I came to understand that whatever people experienced under or because of Nazi rule should be on record at the museum.

While we may want to interpret representations like Anne Frank's diary and Eli Wiesel's *Night* as symbolic and universal, while we don't want to see their experiences as individuated but rather as speaking for many, we have to remember that they are only representing themselves. Here it is useful to recall David Boder's aptly titled book *I Did Not Interview the Dead*, a collection of interviews he conducted in 1946, right after the war, the earliest known interviews with survivors and displaced persons. We must also remember that it is not only the dead we don't interview. We can't interview everyone, and while a particular story may seem representative, we can't know this for sure. Further, some stories are simply more powerful than others because the interviewees are able to speak clearly and vividly about their experiences. Some interviews seem to matter more than others, and I suspect that every interviewer has certain interviews that stay in the mind in detail. For me, my first two interviews, with Bill Lowenberg and Charlene Perlmutter Schiff, became memorable over the years. For me, there is also a cow story, a story about a penknife, a story about singing a lullaby that was sung by a mother, a story about corruption, a story about refusing to say "Heil Hitler," a story about rape or molestation, a story about the Nuremberg Trials, a story about feeding a two-year-old candy so she would make no noise while hiding from a Nazi deportation roundup, a story about a son finding his mother after the war. Actually, the more I think about the interviews, the more stories there are that become unforgettable to me, many more than I originally thought there would be.

Testimonies are about human experience. They demonstrate human subjectivity, not any form of objectivity. They are an attempt to individualize and humanize a story whose dimensions are not accessible to most people, no matter how many voluminous histories they read in an effort to get an overall picture of the events. What grabs most people are the individual stories. They are a source of human reflection more than a recitation of facts and figures. In fact, facts are least likely to be part of an interview. Few people have been in a position to know enough to give us what we can't get from documents. Sometimes individual stories offer personal subjective experiences that supplement documents or written records (although there are exceptions—I don't think there are any documents that could reveal more about the workings of the women's camp at Birkenau than did Zippy Tichauer, debunker of the Mengele myth, in the course of our many conversations). In general, we do not get history from interviews except in a limited biographical sense. We get constructed memories based upon remembered experiences. Oral histories are shaped, whereas experience as it happens is not.

A story, writes Hannah Arendt in her essay on Isak Dinesen in *Men in Dark Times*, "reveals the meaning of what otherwise would remain an unbearable sequence of sheer happenings." We construct stories to fight against an accumulation of sheer happenings that are impossible to live with. Stories help to bring some measure of coherence to our experiences, which would otherwise remain a chronology, not an intelligible picture. We tell stories to make sense of our lives to ourselves and to others. We also create historical narratives to make sense of the larger human history beyond the individual and private. In these ways, we rescue our individual and collective history from oblivion, and in turn history rescues us from sheer happenings, from the isolation of the separate moments in our lives.

We are all familiar with children who have no sense of narrative and simply tell us everything that happened that day—"and then . . . and then . . . and then"—leaving us to wonder, "What's the point?" Some adults do the same thing. Without a narrative to bring some measure of sense to our experiences, they remain a chronology, not a coherent picture. Stories rescue us from the isolation that comes when they remain untold, either because no one wants to hear them or because someone is unable to speak. It is numbing to hear only the itemization of everyday life, with each experience separate from and unconnected to the next. Stories, on the other hand, captivate, fascinate, and teach both the ordinary things of life and the extraordinary.

When someone constructs his or her narrative, we are getting a piece of subjectivity—not a story unrelated to reality but rather a story connected to a person's reflections, a reconstruction that attempts to make sense of events, not in an ultimate but in a proximate way. Such narratives are not usually filled with the sort of facts that please historians, but rather with truths that come from someone thinking about, re-experiencing, and trying to communicate their experiences. The result is a deeply personal and individual story that only partially reveals a larger narrative. Individual narratives are not intended for that purpose. Narrative seems to be a necessity in human life. As I've said, the chronology of our lives usually tells little about us. We need stories to make sense of our individual lives, and we need historical narratives to make sense of human history, beyond our individuality and private experience.

It is crucial to talk about memory with respect to oral history. Because memory is unreliable, many people question the accuracy of oral histories, considering them more suspect than other sources of information. Further, as Holocaust historian Raul Hilberg has mentioned, the oral histories of Holocaust survivors do not represent a random sample of the community that was destroyed. David Boder was right to say that he never interviewed the dead. Whatever witnesses we interview cannot be considered a cross-section of the Jews who were killed or those who survived, which leaves us with another question about the trustworthiness of oral history. What is the place of so-called eyewitness accounts?

I think the question of the value of oral history is related to a larger question about the relationship of biography or autobiography to history. What is interesting here is that paper documents are considered more accurate than oral history, even though paper documents are written by people subject to the same tricks of memory and reliability that we attribute to oral history. It is also the case that using oral history in the reconstruction of history is more labor-intensive than working with documents, many more of which can be read in the time it takes to conduct a single oral history interview. I don't want to say that there are no problems with respect to oral history, and memory is surely one of them, which is why we need to ask a few questions of the survivors we interview. Are they really survivors, are they authentic? Were they in a position to know firsthand about what they tell us? What are the intentions of the interviewees? Why do they want to be interviewed? Does this even matter? What is it that we want to learn about the Holocaust anyway?

When I gave a seminar on oral history at the Holocaust Museum, I remember that Christopher Browning, a historian who had written extensively about the Final Solution and the use of survivor testimony, said two things that seemed contradictory on their face. On the one hand, he said that he would stake his reputation as a historian on the belief "that you can use oral history as a source to create a reliable narrative." He had used oral history in writing about the Starachowice ghetto because there were very few extant documents about that ghetto, so his only choice was to interview survivors. However, when I asked him if he would use oral history again, he said, "Never." The absolutism of his response surprised me, but the viewpoint he expressed is a common one. And I never asked him, "Why never?"

To reiterate, memory is not just a problem for oral history. Other forms of documentation have to be seen as suffering from what might be called memory lapses or lapses in hearing correctly (e.g., notes on meetings or conversations or military orders). Questions about reliability must be asked of any and all sources, including written ones. Does oral history only play an emotional role in the telling of the history of the Holocaust? Can't oral history help us to have a sense of what it was like to be there? Can this only be the job of the historian?

Like narrative, memory is a necessity in human life. Memory sustains continuity, and in the process creates and maintains human identity. If not for memory we would have to construct and/or reconstruct our identity at every moment. Under such circumstances, life would be very strange. Memory is part of what creates the necessary moorings for establishing a history, whether for individuals or groups, because it manages our narratives, and it is in our narratives that we find our historical identity, both private and public. As Luis Buñuel wrote in *My Last Breath*, "Memory is what makes our lives. Life without memory is no life at all.... Our memory is our coherence, our reason, our feeling, even our action. Without it, we are nothing."

While memory may be necessary for our lives, it is not perfect. It doesn't freeze experiences as they are. Or if it does, if it records everything, our capacity to summon all those details is very limited. Neither memories themselves nor the traces of memories in documents and artifacts (e.g., diaries) are necessarily an accurate representation of the past. Documents and artifacts are signposts of an event. They offer perspectives, but never a complete view of an event. Memories also offer perspectives, but again, never a complete view.

Memory is not pure. As Primo Levi says in *The Drowned and the Saved*, "Human memory is a marvelous but fallacious instrument. The memories which lie within us are not carved in stone; not only do they tend to become erased as the years go by, but often they change, or even increase by incorporating extraneous features." Memory, then, is not a faithful or objective reproduction of the past. It is a subjective reconstruction of what has been remembered and what has been forgotten.

Memories are a translation of experience, but they cannot usually provide complete recall because people simply forget parts of their experiences. In memory people consciously or unconsciously select some parts of experience over others. Making a strong moral case for forgetfulness, Nietzsche wrote in *The Use and Abuse of History*, "This is a universal law: a living thing can only be healthy, strong, and productive within a certain horizon. . . . we must know the right time to forget as well as the right time to remember; and instinctively see when it is necessary to feel historically, and when unhistorically. This is the point that the reader is asked to consider; that the unhistorical and the historical are equally necessary to the health of an individual, a community, and a system of culture." As people remember, they consciously and unconsciously distort, hide, neglect, and fabricate as well as heighten memory. Selection, then, is inextricably connected to memory.

We know that the selection process inevitably causes memory to deviate from what actually happened. Some things are overlooked, others are transformed; and then there is the repressed or hidden material. Not surprisingly, memories are often tortured and twisted representations of experience. "All that I was taught at home or at school was colored by denial," writes Susan Griffin in *A Chorus of Stones*, "and thus it became so familiar to me that I did not see it." She continues: "We keep secrets from ourselves that all along we know." It is not simply that human memory is badly trained, but rather that human beings, when possible, incline toward a story that satisfies something other than truth. At the very least, we must forget or de-emphasize some things in order to highlight other things. Recollection involves a process of discrimination among details; our experiences are being ordered in one way or another, even if Eudora Welty is correct that "to the memory nothing is ever lost."

It often seems to me that what has been silenced or left out of an interview may be the most interesting part of the story. Sometimes it only emerges when the camera or tape recorder is off, which is why one interviewer was told by his teacher, "Never turn off the tape recorder." Silence and forgetting are central to the construction of memory. Silence, like forgetfulness, is a partner in the creation of the story. Too many details bring confusion. Too few details give us an inadequate rendition of the experience. If we didn't forget portions of an event, we might not get anything but unrelenting details with no context. Whatever else it may be, forgetfulness is both a problem and a partner in the creation of the story or narrative. Still, we cannot deny that forgetfulness or silences can hide stories, and sometimes these silences hide what is most important or interesting or terrifying.

The mechanisms of memory require silences. Forgetting is a form of silence. If we remember too much, we become paralyzed because we are stuck in the past. But too much forgetting of the past is equally paralyzing because in such a circumstance we become empty. Thus, we live within circles or waves of remembering and forgetting. There is a need for balance between the necessity to forget and the necessity to remember, and while we may have an instinct to do both, we have no instinct for a healthy balance.

To further complicate the process of remembering, memories are influenced by the interpretive suggestions of others. Our personal memories are sometimes countered or contradicted by the views of parents, siblings, lovers, and friends. In this jostling, individuals sometimes add new memories and/or transform old ones.

Potentially more powerful influences over individual memories may hold sway when these memories are attached to "collective remembrances." In such cases the memories of individuals can be outwitted by public expectations and group myths to an even greater degree than in the context of family and friends. The family is a powerful institution, but a group that develops a collective myth often has more tools than a family with which to create or transform an individual's story. In this way personal stories are fit into public remembrances that catapult or ricochet into personal memory, as with the Holocaust survivors' memories of Dr. Mengele or the menstruation stories mentioned earlier.

While memory is one of our ways into the past, at the same time it is a victim of many forces, both personal and political. For instance, it often becomes a casualty of power inequities. Historical reality is distorted not only through the vagaries and weaknesses of the mechanisms of memory itself, but also through conscious and unconscious attempts to conceal memories, and in turn to conceal the experiences of which these memories are traces. All sorts of power structures manage such concealments, perhaps especially power structures that subjugate minorities (e.g., institutionalized racism in the US and elsewhere). In short, as Irene Eber once told me, memory "impinges on events." That is, events can be transformed by how we want to remember them, as well as how we are told to remember them. Consequently, although memory is essential, it is, to repeat, problematic.

Memories linked to experiences of trauma, as in the case of the Holocaust, may be even more problematic than those linked to ordinary experiences. Whatever is unreliable about the remembrance of ordinary events may be more so in the case of events fraught with terror, loss, brutality, and death, where there is even more reason to forget, deny, repress, or cover up than in ordinary life. At the same time, and perhaps for the same reason, there is more cause to remember. In his essay "The Memory of the Offense" (in *The Drowned and the Saved*), Primo Levi writes as follows about the memories of survivors of the Holocaust.

> Even among the victims one can observe a manifold alteration of memories; but in this case there is no deliberate intention to deceive.... It has been observed ... that many former inmates of German camps, or the victims of other traumatic experiences, unconsciously put their memories through a sieve. When invoking them in conversation, they prefer to dwell on the quiet moments, on grotesque or strange or even comical intermezzos, and to skip over the most painful episodes. These last are reluctantly, rarely, recalled from the reservoir of memory; therefore, as time passes by, they tend to fade away and lose their contours.

Levi is calling our attention to those survivors who cannot bear the scrutiny and pain of remembrance and who almost innocently select certain safe or benign memories in order to survive the ordeal in their present circumstances. This selectivity functions to block the pain of what is too awful to remember, to "survive survival," as Irene Eber put it.

This is not to say that survivors of any trauma might not engage in intentional deception, not only because some incidents are simply too painful to keep in full view, but also because they involve guilt or shame over what the survivor did. Victims of the Holocaust do not always see themselves as innocent within the situations constructed by the Nazis. They acted, and in those actions they are not always heroes to themselves. If they consider the actions shameful or if they think others might, intentional deception may well seem a reasonable course.

The real tension between the need to forget and the corollary necessity to remember can lead to the construction of what can only be called an "official memory," a conscious selection of symbols and stories that helps people "survive survival" and locate themselves in a way that their individual tales cannot. Their experiences then become ordered by public memory and validated in the process. Just as an individual can focus on particular memories that transmit meaning, so can groups focus their self-understanding on some particular set of incidents that also symbolize meaning, that presume to bear witness to the events and constitute an identity.

As I have said, whatever our views about the power and limitations of memory, its necessity cannot be denied. Memory is central to our understanding, our construction of identity, both personal and historical. Without it, history loses its grounding. The need to remember or remembrance itself is what prompts history to be transmitted in oral or written form in the first place. Most of us long to know our connections to the past and prefer not to be refugees in our own history.

It is also true that the deeds of human beings, unless remembered, "are the most futile and perishable things on earth," as Hannah Arendt says in *Between Past and Future*. And since we seem to crave some form of immortality, it is clear that our personal history, rather than objects we produce, can only take on an aspect of immortality if we are remembered. It is perhaps for this reason that Mnemosyne, the Greek goddess of remembrance, "was regarded as the mother of all the other muses," Arendt tell us. In order for human deeds to be remembered, they must be embodied in a story that takes us beyond the chronology of sheer occurrence to narrative. And it is because of narrative that we understand William Faulkner's "The past is never dead. It's not even past" (*Requiem for a Nun*), as well as Arendt's "The world we live in at any moment *is* the world of the past. . . . the past *haunts* us; it is the past's function to haunt us who are present and wish to live in the world as it really is, that is, has *become* what it is now" ("Home to Roost," *New York Review of Books*). The problem lies in getting to what "really is," not in the sense of foraging for essences but of trying to get at the important angles and contours of an event or set of events.

Sometimes selectivity is neither benign nor helpful. Sometimes it is deployed to make conscious distortions meant to serve a protective function by establishing cover stories that mock what actually happened. For instance, a few years ago the curator of a Holocaust museum, herself a survivor, told me that she purposely cropped a certain photograph for a Lodz ghetto exhibit. The photo in question showed Jewish children trying to escape a deportation roundup in the ghetto as Jewish policemen grabbed them from their hiding places. She decided to cut the Jewish policeman out of the photo. Those who viewed the exhibit could only see the children being grabbed, not those doing the grabbing. The curator was under the impression that had the actual photograph been shown it would have created or contributed to anti-Semitism, her assumption being that if Jews do not appear to be pure victims, then the horror of the Holocaust is negated. Perhaps she also thought that the original photo might serve to exonerate the Nazis. As Timothy Garton Ash wrote in the *New York Review of Books*, there is "a nationalism of the victim. The nationalism of the victim is one of the many things that Poles and Jews have (or, at least, have had) in common. Characteristic for the nationalism of the victim is a reluctance to acknowledge in just measure the sufferings of other peoples, and an inability to admit that the victim can also victimize." However well intentioned, the curator's decision was harmful. That particular exhibit lied. What this curator did was not the result of the frailties of human memory or a product of the natural limitations of perspective. As a survivor she had a stake in not telling part of the story. This is only one small example of how a set of facts and memories can be ignored in favor of creating an "official memory" that transforms and deforms a set of events.

In spite of what I have said about the necessity of memory, I sometimes wonder whether it does any good to remember. I am not saying that it isn't good to remember; as Susan Sontag puts it in *Against Interpretation and Other Essays*, "We acknowledge that the Holocaust is, in some sense, incomprehensible. Ultimately, the only response is to continue to hold the events in mind. . . . we may feel that it is *right* or fitting, or proper" to remember. I am not questioning this; rather, I am asking another question: whether remembering makes any difference politically or morally. If the memory of the Holocaust changes nothing, then why remember? To be clear, I am emphatically not saying that the Holocaust changed nothing—I believe it changed the history of Western civilization. I am simply asking whether our recollection of it makes it possible for us to be different from those who participated in the Holocaust, in other words, to prevent genocide. Does memory ensure that the phrase "Never again" means something?

The role of the interviewer is that of an awakener of memories or a questioner who brings the memory back to what it knows. An interviewee's memory is a shadow of the past, a representation of what happened. In Plato's Allegory of the Cave, prisoners are chained to a wall and can see nothing but the shadows cast on that wall, which they take to be reality. One prisoner is freed and goes out into the world, then returns and tries to convince the other prisoners that the shadows are not reality at all, but they are reluctant to believe and leave the only life they've known. Our role as interviewers is different from that of Plato's freed prisoner: it is not to show the truth to interviewees but rather to pose questions, to provide a setting in which they can tell us about their experiences. As with the freed prisoner, we attempt to bring memories into light without too much trauma, yet there is often no other way to get at the truth of their experiences.

As interviewers, we try to travel with our interviewees. We try to see more than their representations. We try to understand from the inside as if we were there, much like a musician trying to inhabit a piece of music. We try to sit within the person's story as if nothing else exists, and we try to understand. But we are always removed, even if we are not always distant. If an interviewer helps release the story of the interviewee through the questions, through this special relationship, the interviewer too is released into another world. The interviewer then becomes the student; the interviewee becomes the teacher. We all live in a world of shadows, and the attempt here is to bring some light, some understanding from the dialogue.

In discussing the meaning of the Socratic dialectic, Hannah Arendt wrote that "thinking is the silent dialogue with oneself." We might see interviewing as an attempt to bring the thinking and feeling self out of this silence. Interviewers try to get beneath the surface memory or the official memory or the collective memory. It might be said that we want, somehow, to trick the already selected memory to go beyond itself.

The creation of the story of experiences, whether during the Holocaust or at any other time, is a process of forgetting and remembering. It depends upon the questions asked of oneself or by another in dialogue, questions that allow the memory its freedom to speak. The primary value of oral histories lies in the details they reveal about individual personal experience. Most recorded testimonies were produced long after the events occurred. Hence, there are always concerns about the accuracy of any given report. Memory is certainly fallible. Although concerns about accuracy can be well founded, it is also true that these eyewitness testimonies, no matter how far away from an event, offer a window into experiences that almost no historical writing can offer. These testimonies, personal and individual, emotionally draw us into a story whose historical outlines often feel impenetrable. The individual testimony is accessible and creates the possibility of understanding the

Holocaust in ways that historical analysis cannot. This is not to say that testimony takes the place of historical analysis. It is rather to claim that testimony has its own important place next to historical analysis.

Storytelling is always powerful. Oral history in one form or another is one of the oldest forms of documentation in human history. It is one of the oldest forms of educating. We have new forms, new media through which the human voice and face are transmitted. But it is the human face, the human voice, the human story that remain at the core. We can transmit more readily, keep the transmission for many years, but the question remains: What do we want to tell? That question stayed with me throughout my tenure as director of oral history.

When I first took the job, I was afraid that I didn't have sufficient imagination for this work. Not only did doing interviews on video feel daunting, but I wondered whether I could think of projects for the department that went beyond interviewing survivors about their experiences during the Holocaust. Over time, I did come up with a number of projects, some of which may even have demonstrated a spark of imagination.

Before the opening of the museum in April 1993, there were no finding aids—a technical term meaning detailed inventories and descriptions of the contents of an archive so that information can be easily ac-cessed—for the two hundred or so interviews with survivors that had already been conducted, much less for future interviews. I rounded up half a dozen interns to write up summaries of the interviews so that there would at least be some immediate way for people to locate in-terviews of interest. I also began the process of writing up guidelines for our work, which eventually became a 140-page document titled *Oral History Interview Guidelines*, first published in 1998, revised in 2007, and still available on the USHMM website.

I was also involved with two projects that addressed the question

"What do we want to tell?" and that remain unique to the museum's Oral History Department, as far as I know. One had to do with bringing together interviewers from National Public Radio to do audio interviews with survivors about their lives after the Holocaust. We had already done video interviews with these survivors about their experiences during the Holocaust, but the point here was to ask them how they had coped afterward, how they had "survived survival," in Irene Eber's words. Neenah Ellis, an NPR producer and a close friend (the one who helped me buy my Steinway, as recounted in my first essay), set us up with some NPR interviewers, and we constructed a two-day seminar to talk about the project. We explained that each potential interviewer would be required to watch my video interview with Charlene Perlmutter Schiff as an example that might help them understand what survivors had gone through, what it might take to interview a survivor about such experiences, and how they might frame the questions they would ask in an audio interview about a survivor's life after the Holocaust. We also gave them some suggestions included in the *Oral History Interview Guidelines*. The result was more than 130 interviews, some of which became the basis for the Holocaust Museum's website Life After the Holocaust.

The final project was the Perpetrators, Collaborators and Witnesses Documentation Project, started in 1999 after I met with potential museum donors Jeff and Toby Herr, who were unusual because they were specifically interested in oral history. In our discussions, Toby suggested that we interview non-Jews about their involvement with the Holocaust, and I thought it was a good idea. I recall that she asked me whether I was truly interested and that I told her I really didn't want money for projects I couldn't support. The Herrs ended up giving us a million dollars. I hired Nathan Beyrak, an Israeli who I thought could actually handle this complex and difficult project, and I believe I was quite correct to do so. Nathan had the courage and the chutzpah to go to various European countries in search of witnesses, collaborators, and perpetrators. I don't know anyone who could have done a better job, although I must admit to one difficult discussion with him about his decision to focus solely on what non-Jewish people saw or did with respect to Jewish persecution, with no attempt to get a kind of life picture of them, as we did with Jewish survivors. Nathan clearly did not care for these people and so was not curious about the larger context of their history. Perhaps of more significance, he also told me that they would not agree to talk on video for a lengthy interview, so my idea of what an interview should be did not fit his reality on the ground. I accepted his position even though I wished it had been otherwise.

I invited the Shoah Foundation and the Fortunoff Video Archive for Holocaust Testimonies at Yale to join us in this project and was refused by both. I particularly remember that the head of the Fortunoff collection seemed to think that we were proposing to pay perpetrators for their testimony and they wanted no part of such an exchange. I said that we never paid anyone for an interview and that we would most likely be interviewing witnesses, not collaborators or perpetrators, and that the only cost we might incur was for travel expenses, as we would for a survivor. That didn't seem to matter. We continued without the support of the Shoah Foundation and the Fortunoff Video Archive for Holocaust Testimonies at Yale. Since its inception in 1999, the Perpetrators, Collaborators and Witnesses Documentation Project, which is ongoing, has produced some 2,700 valuable interviews from fifteen countries. These interviews, which can be found at the Jeff and Toby Herr Oral History Archive at the museum, are primarily interviews with witnesses, although we managed to interview some perpetrators and collaborators.

There is no redemptive meaning to be found in the Holocaust. In a deep way, it may always remain "incomprehensible" to use Susan Sontag's word. Still, if we are to understand the century in which it occurred, if we are to know what this history portends for humanity, if we are to be at home in or familiar with this world, we must know about the Holocaust, and one of the ways to know about it is through the stories and memories of those who were there. Remembering, even if it doesn't help to prevent genocide, is a moral obligation and a moral good. Remembering may not be enough to prevent genocide, but it is a necessary condition for the actions necessary to prevent genocide, and thus a necessary condition for the injunction "Never again."

FIVE

Sarajevo

> In the dark times,
> will there also be singing?
> Yes, there will be singing.
> About the dark times.
> —Bertolt Brecht, "Motto"

It is no longer a surprise that genocide is an intimate companion of war. Among other genocides, two took place in Europe in the twentieth century: one has a name, the other does not. The first is the Holocaust, or Shoah, which occurred in the context of a war of aggression waged by Germany under the Nazi regime. The second occurred in the context of a war of aggression waged by Serbia in the former Yugoslavia, primarily against Bosnians. Naming takes time.

Both events are part of my life. As a teenager, I learned that my father's parents, his younger brother, and some eighty other members of his family had been killed during the Holocaust, and that was my first connection to it. I began to feel that the fact of my having been born in the United States in 1939 was a lucky accident; had I been born in Europe,

I probably would not have survived World War II. This realization gave me a sense of moral obligation to spend part of my life learning as much as I could about what happened during the Holocaust. Many years later, I decided to pursue a graduate degree in philosophy, a field that did not often deal with matters of genocide, prejudice, oppression, and racism, but I knew that my courses would when I began teaching.

By 1992, I was working at the United States Holocaust Memorial Museum, and when the siege of Sarajevo began that April, a form of paralysis embraced some of us who were organizing the museum's Permanent Exhibition. The meaning of "ethnic cleansing" became clear after the television and print reports about the deluge of refugees, after the discovery of the concentration camps at Omarska, Manjača, and Sanski Most, after documentation of the mass killings of civilians and the systematic rapes. At that point, the connection with World War II and the Holocaust seemed inescapable, and a contradiction emerged in our work at the museum. How could we devote ourselves to the history of one genocide while watching another one on television? How could we maintain our everyday routines while genocide was being perpetrated in Bosnia? If we ignored what was happening there, weren't we the equivalent of the witnesses or bystanders we implicitly criticized throughout the Permanent Exhibition? We had an abundance of moral indignation, political analysis, and sadness. Many in the museum administration saw no problem, and eventually those of us who did went on with our work anyway.

In order to work, we had to forget. Or, to put it another way, we had to silence the war and the genocide in Bosnia when we worked. Some of us signed petitions. Some marched or spoke at rallies. Some joined organizations protesting what was seen as culpable inaction on the part of the United States, the United Nations, and the European Community. No matter. The conflict persisted, both in Bosnia and at the museum. We wanted our work to have moral and political meaning. We hoped the museum would have an impact on those who visited.

The words "Never again," a mantra at the museum, seemed to be words of action, but it was clear that whatever else we were doing, nothing we did at this museum at this moment would stop the war and genocide in Bosnia. We had no power. We went on.

In August 1992, the museum did put out a good press release that made comparisons between the Holocaust and what was happening in Bosnia. It also made a significant and, for some of us, a mistaken claim: that the museum's mandate "is history, not politics." Still, the press release urged governments to take action "to bring safety and relief to the civilian victims of the Serbian government's calculated, deliberately inhuman campaign."

In April 1993, at the opening of the Holocaust Museum, Elie Wiesel spoke. At one point he turned to President Clinton and made an impassioned plea on behalf of Bosnia: "As a Jew, I am saying that we must do something to stop the bloodshed in that country! People fight each other and children die. Why? Something, anything must be done." Although Wiesel accused no one, mentioned nothing really specific, his words provoked applause and relief in some quarters. At least someone had said something. Heads of state from all over the world had been invited to the opening ceremony, but not the government of Serbia, and when the name of the president of Croatia was announced, strong boos were heard from the crowd.

Not until August 1995 did the museum issue a second press release about the situation in Bosnia. The language was more general this time. No longer was Serbia mentioned, no longer were the primary victims named, which made the press release problematic to many. Still, the United States Holocaust Memorial Museum had said something, however inadequate.

When you emerge from the museum's Permanent Exhibition, you see these words from Elie Wiesel: "For the dead *and* the living we must bear witness." We are to bear witness and to remember in order not to repeat the mistakes of the past, to paraphrase George Santayana's famous line, by now a cliché.

Which raises a number of questions to which I have no answers. Suppose we discover that even if we do remember, it doesn't make much difference? Then what? What are we supposed to do with memory anyway? What is supposed to happen when the memory of the past confronts the present? What can we expect from memory, from memorials, from books, from documentaries, from news accounts about such tragedies as the Holocaust, the genocides in Bosnia, Cambodia, Rwanda, and innumerable other instances of mass murder and gross suffering? What are those who were there supposed to do? What are those who were not there supposed to do? How big is the shadow of the Holocaust? Does the Holocaust illuminate? If so, what does it illuminate?

In late 1993, I began to meet people from Sarajevo, first Suada Kapić and then Haris Pašović, who invited me to travel there and speak. However, it was not until well after the Dayton Accords were agreed in November 1995, ending the war, that this trip took place, on the occasion of an event held in September 1996, where the Holocaust was to be the focus of a weekend of programs. The film *Shoah,* directed by Claude Lanzmann, was scheduled to be shown on Bosnian television, and Lanzmann agreed to come and discuss his work. Susan Sontag also agreed to come but in the end could not. I was hesitant to be in such illustrious company, but Suada and Haris wouldn't hear of my doubts, so I agreed to give a talk entitled "Memory and Silence: Remembering and Forgetting."

Some of my colleagues at the museum didn't understand my acceptance of the invitation. Their voices were filled with incredulity or alarm when they asked, "*Why* are you going?" Because I wanted to and needed to, I told them. I felt an obligation to make the journey. It was an obligation I'd carried for almost three years, ever since those first hours I spent with Suada, who had lived in Sarajevo through the siege and who became my friend. To travel to Sarajevo during the siege would have been a way to make a strong statement on the side of the Bosnians and against the aggression being perpetrated primarily by Serbia, but I couldn't do it because I was afraid. Ari Roth, a theater director, had also been invited during the siege. We talked together in my office for a long time, and he too decided not to go because of the danger. Now, when the invitation came after the war, the trip felt imperative. Perhaps naïvely, I was not afraid for my physical safety because the war was over, a view not shared by family and friends. Even if their judgments seemed reasonable, I had to ignore them lest they deter me from going.

Still, I was apprehensive. A trip to this place of so many recent and continuing war crimes provoked deep anxiety, which in part had to do with my lecture. Never had it seemed so hard to picture the room, the audience, the situation, as I was trying to figure out what to say. I had never been in a war or a war zone, never been a target of mass murderers or snipers, never been a refugee. Although not abstract, my experience of war and genocide was either secondhand or theoretical. What could I possibly offer to those who had lost so much during the siege of Sarajevo and the war in Bosnia?

I was also worried about whether I could subdue my inclination to connect the events in the former Yugoslavia too much with the Holocaust. Would everything in Sarajevo remind me of the Holocaust—every destroyed or damaged building, every person's story, every grave? I wanted to hear what Bosnians had to say about their lives without perpetually calling up the words and images of Holocaust survivors. I felt that the importance of the events in Bosnia should not be diminished by seeing them only in light of the Holocaust or by transforming them into the equivalent of the Holocaust in order to justify their importance. In my view, such comparisons accomplished nothing if I wished to know and understand the particularity of this history. Still, not drawing on my knowledge of the Holocaust was going to be difficult, if not impossible

I think there was another level of anxiety linked to my desire and need to go to Sarajevo. There are a few books on the Holocaust that seem to put you in such close proximity to what happened that you cannot bear to read more than a few lines at a time. There are certain testimonies of survivors or witnesses to the Holocaust that also create this feeling of proximity, if only the proximity to memory or the memory of memory. In preparing for the trip to Sarajevo, I knew that I would be in greater proximity to a locale of genocide than I had ever been before, even when I visited Auschwitz-Birkenau, and I did not know what this would mean. How would I respond to what I saw, heard, and felt in Sarajevo? I was not physically afraid, I was ontologically afraid. I was afraid to hear about what happened while being where it all happened. I was afraid that the protective distance of time and circumstance I had in my work on the Holocaust would not protect me in Sarajevo.

I took my first and only trip to Auschwitz in 1989, traveling from Berlin with three new friends from Germany. In spite of all my study, I had never visited a concentration or extermination camp before. There wasn't much to see in Auschwitz, and yet there was so much to take in. The buildings, or what was left of them, were in various stages of deterioration. There were no visitors that day, no docents to lead us through the desolate space. It felt like a world of nothingness where only silence spoke or the dead spoke through the silence. We didn't talk much as we walked and walked, though we had all studied this place and those times. Rain soaked our coats, mud caked our shoes, and we remembered survivors' descriptions of the unforgiving weather. It was an extremely powerful couple of days, but it was forty-four years after the liberation of Auschwitz-Birkenau, forty-four years after the end of the war. The impact came from an accumulation of study as well as conversations with survivors, not so much from what we saw— the impact came from what we already knew. Although the room filled with piles of shorn hair took our breath away, we already knew we would encounter it.

The trip to Sarajevo was different. Everything about the war, the siege, the genocide was fresh. Everyone I met lived in the shadow of what they had experienced. Life had not yet been reconstructed. The shooting had stopped; the war remained. When people spoke, it was not from the distant past. They spoke with immediacy. I don't know if memory is more accurate in that context; I only know it felt different from listening to the testimonies of Holocaust survivors. Perhaps I knew intellectually that this must be so, but before this short trip to Sarajevo, I had no experience of that difference.

As we flew into Sarajevo, I could see ruins everywhere. Bits and pieces of walls were all that remained of what had been buildings. If you didn't know there had been a war, you might have thought you were looking at ruins from an ancient era. In 1996 the Sarajevo airport was uninviting and stark, a steel grey structure twisted by shells and surrounded by destroyed buildings and dirt roads. No formal entry awaited us, no ritual of customs, no officials stamping passports. We walked to an exit point on one of the dirt roads and found a steel chain through which we could pass once we had identified our luggage, although there was no one there to check our luggage tags. On the other side of the chain stood a familiar face, Haris Pašović, and some young people I didn't know.

On our way to the car that would take us into the city proper, one of the young people said that this wonderful new road had been nothing but mud during the siege. It was a dirt road to me, but I was given to understand that it was a vast improvement over the former mud road. The buildings that still stood near the airport were uninhabitable, pocked with holes from bombs, mortar shells, and bullets.

Sarajevo gave the impression of a city that had been wrecked and driven back in time. Among other harrowing sights was a melted steel structure that looked as if it had collapsed in on itself. It had housed the offices of the newspaper *Oslobodjenje,* published daily during the siege, with the staff operating out of the basement after the building was destroyed. I had seen photographs of the siege, and I had seen the Survival Map of Sarajevo (conceived by Suada Kapić), which showed the lines of the Yugoslav People's Army and their Bosnian Serb allies surrounding the city, tank emplacements, paths for avoiding snipers, places to get water and wood. Pictures may be worth a thousand words, but of course the place itself revealed more than the best of pictures. Being there, I could feel the narrow confines of the city under siege. Although there was reconstruction here and there, UN blue plastic still covered many windows blown out by the shelling. There was broken glass everywhere, and I could still see the craters left by grenades, sometimes identified by red paint or a red waxlike substance. As far as I could see, Sarajevo was almost bare of trees; most of them had been cut down for firewood.

Unlike Auschwitz-Birkenau, Sarajevo was not uninhabited and barren. People filled the streets, coffeehouses, trolleys, taxicabs, and shops. Children were in school. Some university classes were in session. Residents walked their puppies and pushed their babies in strollers on the west side of the Miljacka River, which flows through the center of the city. Somehow the river seemed aggressive to me, so that it was difficult to believe that Enes Sivac's sculptures *Flying Man* and *Cyclist* (now called *Equilibrists*) had ever presided over it as a symbol of cultural resistance. (More appropriate to the way I was feeling might have been Annie Liebovitz's famous photograph *Bloody Bicycle,* taken during a trip to Sarajevo in 1993 after a boy riding his bike near her car was hit by a mortar and killed.) I saw poor people scavenging for food in garbage cans, but no one on crutches or in wheelchairs, which seemed odd to me given the violence of the war. I particularly remember the skeletal building that had been the national library. There were no books there, just a cavernous space with shattered walls.

I was walking that day with Suada, who expressed shock at seeing lights on in buildings and cars on the road, and especially at walking without being in the range of snipers. Later I went down a dark staircase on Tita Street while holding the arm of a new acquaintance, Senada, who was to do the simultaneous translation of my talk. I could see nothing. The moment reminded her of how it was during the siege and how she learned to negotiate the dark. "Sarajevo during the siege was like living in a tomb," she said.

It occurred to me that Sarajevo under siege must have resembled some combination of ghetto, concentration camp, and shooting gallery. After walking the streets of the city, I began to have a visceral understanding of some of what its people had lived through. I had not been able to visualize properly the geography and situation of the city until I walked its streets and saw the view of the surrounding mountains and went to those mountains and saw a sniper's view of the city. I was glad I'd had a limited understanding of Sniper Alley before I came to Sarajevo, because I'd known my friends walked there every day. Although I really thought I understood, I hadn't fully imagined their vulnerability on every corner, in each doorway, in every bed, in every inch of that city. The possibility of being killed or wounded was omnipresent.

Each encounter with a Sarajevan offered a tale about the siege: where to get water or what happened when you tried; where to buy cigarettes; what food was eaten or craved; the massacres, the deaths, the near misses (e.g., a hole in a coat from a bullet that had missed the wearer's flesh); the boredom, the despair, the anger, the humor, the passions; the impossibility of work, and still the everyday trips to the office; washing clothes in an impossibly small office sink and carrying the wet, heavy clothes back home. People would walk to stay sane, or because a walk represented life or freedom in spite of the constant danger from shells and snipers, and on those walks they might see the devastating, paralyzing sight of bodies and body parts on the streets or in the park. Then there were those who had never identified as Muslims but rather as Yugoslavs; now they were identified as Muslims by the aggressors, and sometimes by themselves. And there were artists, musicians, actors, and others who continued to produce and perform in spite of the siege.

In Sarajevo in 1996, everything about the war, the siege, the genocide was immediate. Though the active shooting had stopped, everyone was living in the shadow of what they had experienced. The war was not a memory, it was present. When people spoke, it was not from the distant past. Because they were still in the experience, their recounting had an intensity different from the intensity of those telling their stories years and miles away from where the events occurred. Their experiences didn't happen "over there"; they happened here.

For example, during a walk with Suada, she stopped to show me a marketplace that had been bombed in August 1995, killing more than forty people and injuring many more. She recounted what I already knew from a letter she'd sent me—that she had been in that very spot only minutes before the bomb went off. "I'm not superstitious," she said, "but I'm convinced that the Hamsa charm you sent me saved my life." I couldn't speak. I'm not superstitious either, but I was glad I'd sent her the Hamsa. We paused at this spot in silence.

Although I knew the story of my friend's near miss and had seen the aftermath of the massacre on television, the immediacy of the locale changed the impact of the story. As obvious as it sounds, it was a different reality than any of the photographs, documentaries, and news reports could convey—different to see the spot, to feel the dimensions of the place, to know firsthand the proximity of mountains filled with snipers and tanks, to talk with someone who was there then and was standing beside me now in the same place. To be there with Suada chilled me.

Life in Sarajevo at the time of my visit was suspended between the past and a completely uncertain future, between a siege that made no sense and an aftermath that resolved little or nothing. This was a pivotal and fragile moment to be in the company of the people of Sarajevo. I had thought that my reading about the Holocaust and the former Yugoslavia, as well as my relationships with Holocaust survivors, would prepare me intellectually and emotionally for what I might encounter, but I was wrong.

Until I went to Sarajevo, my closest experience with genocide was that trip to Auschwitz-Birkenau in 1989. However overwhelming it was, it took place forty-four years after the camp was liberated. There were no bodies of victims, no survivors needing help or wanting to talk, no stench. The detritus of war and genocide was nowhere to be seen. There was only the silence and our memories of the stories my companions and I had heard from people who were there. I had never spoken with a Holocaust survivor in a Displaced Persons camp in 1945 or 1946. I had never walked through Auschwitz, the Warsaw ghetto, or Krakow right after war. I had imagined what it was like, but all I'd seen of those places at that time were photos and documentary footage. I did not interview the survivors in the immediate aftermath of the war and the genocide, I did not hear their tone of voice, their anger, despair, intensity, hope, and fear. In Sarajevo, though I tried to avoid comparisons, it was inevitable that I would turn to what I had studied, thought, and felt about the Holocaust. The Holocaust was not my experience, but it is part of my own shadow. After my few days in Sarajevo, the city became part of my shadow too. The Holocaust helped me to understand Sarajevo, and Sarajevo helped me to understand the Holocaust, but in both cases my understanding was incomplete.

I knew that my life experiences and the experiences of my friends in Sarajevo were worlds apart. I was an outsider, and I remained an outsider, even as an invited guest (or an "American Aunt," as I was sometimes called). That didn't make my concern, my capacity for understanding, my study of this history any less authentic, but it did mean that while I was closer in time to the experiences of people who suffered, I was not closer to the experiences themselves. They lived through the siege, I did not; I read about it. They endured the terror, the hunger, the betrayal, the loneliness, the bullets, the shells, I did not; I read about it. My experience with genocide was a history of theory, of books, of stories told to me by others. The genocide was their experience, not mine. No amount of reading, no capacity for empathy or sympathy changed that.

Still, I had crossed a line into the suspended space between the past and the future. For a few days, I walked with those whose lives were enmeshed in the transition, or in the attempt at a transition, whose stories and lives had not yet been not reconstructed. It was as if they were walking down dark stairs without a banister, to paraphrase the title of Hannah Arendt's *Thinking Without a Banister*. It was there, on those dark stairs, in those dark times, that I caught a glimpse of a space I had only read about.

In spite of the bustle of people and the evident reconstruction in some parts of the city, life was not normal. How long does it take to get used to a siege? How long to get used to not having gas or electricity or running water, sufficient food, your own apartment, warmth? What does it take to live with the knowledge that you can be killed at any moment because someone is targeting you? What does it take to live with the knowledge that your family, your best friend, your lover can be killed at any moment? And how long does it take to get used to the end of a siege? What does it take to get back to normal? Is that even possible after such a radical break with life as it was?

On my second day in Sarajevo, I gave my talk, "Memory and Silence: Remembering and Forgetting," simultaneously translated into Bosnian by Senada. We were in a small classroom at the law school of Sarajevo University, with chairs and desks configured into a square so we could see the audience of twenty-five or so people. Claude Lanzmann sat to my left, Haris Pašović to my right. Since much of my talk covered ground I've already covered in previous essays in this book, especially "Oral History," I've condensed and paraphrased it here rather than quoting it directly. I have also left much of the second and third parts of the talk in the present tense as though I were addressing you, the reader, as though you had been there in that small room.

I began by saying that I had never been in a war or a war zone, had never been a target of mass murder, although members of my family were, that I only knew about war, mass murder, and genocide from talking to people who were there, from the interviews I watched and conducted, from books, documents, documentary footage, films, and photos. I said that my primary research on genocide had been the Holocaust of World War II, with an emphasis on women's experiences. I said I'd read a good deal and watched documentaries about what happened here during the war, during the genocide, that I'd talked with a few people who had lived through the siege and the war, that I'd tried to think and to act, but since I had not been here, I had only the slightest idea, a semblance of imagination, about what they had endured and what they were living with now.

I told the audience about my work at the Holocaust Museum and the dilemmas the Bosnian war had raised for some of us organizing the Permanent Exhibition. In spite of the words "Never again," I had been naïve to think that protests by the museum's employees would effect change, much less that a federal agency like the museum would take action that its own government was unwilling to take. I concluded the first part of my talk by reading a passage from David Rieff's *Slaughterhouse: Bosnia and the Failure of the West.*

It is hard to be dispassionate about ethnic cleansing and mass murder. After a few visits to Bosnia, I wanted to be nowhere else. Before long, I had put everything else on hold, resolved to write as frankly incendiary a narrative as I could about my journeys to the slaughterhouse that the Republic of Bosnia-Herzegovina became in the spring of 1992. If the bad news about Bosnia could just be brought home to people, I remember thinking, the slaughter would not be allowed to continue.

In retrospect, I should have known better than to believe in the power of unarmed truths. The skies did not darken over Auschwitz and they would not darken over the hills of Bosnia.

After a break and a discussion period in which people recounted their personal experiences during the siege, I went on with the second part of my talk. I spoke of the balance between memory and forgetting, of the tension between the necessity to remember and the need to forget, of memory and silence, of the selectivity of memory in its ordering of experience and its susceptibility to mistakes, conscious or unconscious distortions, and suppressions of the painful or ugly. I read a long quote from Charlotte Delbo, a gentile sent to Auschwitz for her activities in the French resistance, perhaps best known for her memoir *None of Us Will Return*, here writing in her collection *Days and Memory*, published in 1985, forty years after the liberation of the camp.

Auschwitz is so deeply etched in my memory that I cannot forget one moment of it.—So you are living with Auschwitz?—No I live next to it. Auschwitz is there, unalterable, precise, but enveloped in the skin of memory, an impermeable skin that isolates it from my present self. Unlike the snake's skin, the skin of memory does not renew itself. Oh, it may harden further....Alas, I often fear lest it grow thin, crack, and the camp get hold of me again. Thinking about it makes me tremble with apprehension....

Over dreams the conscious will has no power....And in those dreams I see myself, yes, my own self such as I know I was. ... the suffering I feel is so unbearable, so identical to the pain endured there, that I feel it physically, I feel it throughout my whole body which becomes a mass of suffering; and I feel death fasten on me, I feel that I am dying. Luckily, in my agony I cry out. My cry wakes me and I emerge from the nightmare, drained. It takes days for everything to get back to normal, for everything to get shoved back inside memory, and for the skin of memory to mend again. I become myself again, the person you know, who can talk to you about Auschwitz without exhibiting or registering any anxiety or emotion. Because when I talk to you about Auschwitz, it is not from deep memory my words issue. They come from external memory . . . from intellectual memory, the memory connected with thinking processes. Deep memory preserves sensations, physical imprints. It is the memory of the senses.

What is clear from this and other testimonies is that even if most survivors can't or won't express themselves as directly as Delbo does, they always live side by side with their memories, if not inside them, and that these memories allow neither integration nor solace in the present. How could anyone manage to accommodate the facts of the Holocaust in their own experience? Thus, the past, especially the traumatic past, lives side by side with the present.

I am sure that the memories of the survivors were different immediately after the war than they are now. At liberation the separation between past and present was less pronounced. This was a time not only to reconstruct life but also to figure out what really happened in order to construct memory and to try to understand.

Primo Levi describes in *The Drowned and the Saved* the process of silencing in survivors and perpetrators: "A person who has been wounded tends to block out the memory so as not to renew the pain; the person who has inflicted the wound pushes the memory deep down, to be rid of it, to alleviate the feeling of guilt." Raul Hilberg, a prominent Holocaust historian, once said in a lecture that the perpetrators used euphemisms in speaking of what they did ("resettlement," "deportation," "final solution"—now we have "ethnic cleansing") and rarely said, "I am now killing or I have killed women and children and men." He added: "Such direct descriptions might have forced them to confront their conscience." This is probably a stretch.

Those who were there in the Holocaust of World War II, or in the war and slaughter in Bosnia, Rwanda, or Cambodia, cannot completely turn away from their memories, no matter how much they engage in repression. Victims cannot turn away with the ease of those of us who were not there. And so we create memory with silences that speak and silences that do not. In the words of Isak Dinesen, as quoted by Hannah Arendt, in *Men in Dark Times*, "When the storyteller is loyal... to the story, there, in the end, silence will speak. When the story has been betrayed, silence is but emptiness. But we, the faithful, when we have spoken our last word, will hear the voice of silence." I was not there during the Holocaust, and hence I can close a book about it or shut off the TV or walk out of the Holocaust Museum without seeing the entire exhibition. When I come home from doing an interview with a Holocaust survivor, I remember the interview, but I don't live in it, and if I live with it for a while, the memory of the interview usually recedes. Of course this is not equivalent to survivors who remember the experience as it happened to them. While I am experiencing the memory of an interview, they are re-experiencing a part of their lives.

Those of us at the United States Holocaust Memorial Museum could stay in our comfort zone even while facing the horrible pictures from Bosnia, hearing the gruesome stories, or watching the documentary footage. We balanced remembering and forgetting, and in the process we silenced Bosnia so we could work. Thus, while it may be necessary to remember the Holocaust, it may not do any good. We may not have forgotten Bosnia, but we didn't let it drag us away from our work and our everyday lives. We became long-distance bystanders. We learned, if we didn't already know it, that studying the Holocaust or being a survivor of the Holocaust doesn't make a person moral, or morally or politically active.

With that dispiriting observation, I concluded the second part of my talk. Another break and more discussion ensued before I went on with Part III, "Memory as Story or the Story in Memory," which I began by quoting the Spanish filmmaker Luis Buñuel in his memoir *My Last Breath*: "Memory is what makes our lives. . . . Our memory is our coherence, our reason, our feeling, even our action. Without it, we are nothing."

It isn't sheer memory that seems most compelling, except when we lose it. Rather it is the narrative that memory creates or the story that memory produces. Writing in the *New Yorker,* in his article "The Neurologist's Notebook: Prodigies," Oliver Sacks speaks of the memory of autistic savants.

> The large and the small, the trivial and the momentous, may be indifferently mixed, without any sense of salience, of foreground versus background. There is little disposition to generalize from these particulars, or to integrate them with each other, causally or historically, or with the self. In such a memory there tends to be an immovable connection of scene and time, of content and context (a so-called concrete-situational, or episodic, memory).

This lack of connection, of generalization, is what Hannah Arendt refers to when she says in her essay on Isak Dinesen in *Men in Dark Times,* "The story reveals the meaning of what otherwise would remain an unbearable sequence of sheer happenings." Which is to say that without the story, we would have separate pieces, isolated moments, and no possibility of a history, personal or otherwise.

I would like to talk now about the US Holocaust Memorial Museum and its Permanent Exhibition, which is an attempt to tell a complex story. Within its narrative structure (primarily about the Jews but also including other victim groups), there are two spaces where those who were there and survived can be heard directly. These two spaces—the Audio Theater's "Voices from Auschwitz" and the *Testimony* film—are among the most intimate in the museum, especially *Testimony* at the end of the entire exhibition.

Somehow these spaces humanize the exhibition and make what happened more compelling. Putting a human face on the Holocaust diminishes distance. In *Testimony* the stories don't change the horror, they don't romanticize the events, they don't allow for a happy ending, yet people are touched in ways that seem to make it easier for them to leave the museum. Alongside the historical memory they've acquired from the museum's narrative, they've now had an emotional encounter with the testimonies of individuals. Perhaps it is a relief to see that at least some survived and can talk about it. These few who survived tell stories that evoke the history seen in the exhibition because each story also harbors the tragedies of that history.

Isak Dinesen says that if we are loyal to the story, silence will speak. But what does it mean to be loyal to the story? What is the story anyway? There is always more than one story to tell, so the question becomes which should be transmitted. What are the stories that give us what we should know or that tell us how it was? History is filled with differing points of view as to what the story really is.

There was a struggle at the museum about how to maintain the narrative flow about the largest group of Holocaust victims, the Jews, while respecting the suffering and murder of other groups: homosexuals, Jehovah's Witnesses, Roma and Sinti, political prisoners, Russian POWs, the mentally and physically handicapped subjected to euthanasia. There were arguments about how to portray the perpetrators. Should we do so primarily by showing what they did and to whom, or should we give them a human face by telling something about their histories as well as their work for the Nazis? And what about prior genocides, like the genocide against the Armenians? What about post-Holocaust genocides? What about subgroups within the victim groups, like women?

Some at the museum wanted to create a Women's Room that would display the hair shaved from women in Auschwitz. I and others argued against such a ghettoization of women and for the inclusion of shaven hair in the Permanent Exhibition. We lost the battle. There was no actual hair in the exhibition, only a picture of it, and no direct information about gender and its implications. At the time, most scholars erased or ignored gender, and so did the museum.

Imagine for a moment that the systematic rape of Bosnian women were to be ignored in the narrative of the war in the former Yugoslavia. Can the war be told truthfully without these rapes? The genocide against the Jews may have been the first time in history that women and children were targeted for destruction along with men, perhaps the first time that women were not taken as spoils but were to be killed just like men. The fact of gender differentiation suggests that for men and women what happened was not the same. Being loyal to the story is not always easy or possible.

In the final part of my talk, I returned to the issue of what good it does to remember and whether history is healing. What can we expect when we tell stories? What can we expect when we tell the story of the Holocaust? When we tell the story of the siege of Sarajevo, of the war in Bosnia-Herzegovina? We can expect nothing. As Hanna Arendt writes in her essay on the philosopher Lessing in *Men in Dark Times*, "The best that can be achieved is to know precisely what it [the past] was, and to endure this knowledge, and then to wait and see what comes of knowing and enduring. . . . Insofar as any 'mastering' of the past is possible, it consists in relating what has happened; but such narration, too, which shapes history, solves no problems and assuages no suffering; it does not master anything once and for all."

We can never predict whether knowledge of the story of the Holocaust will change anything. But one thing is for sure, if we don't speak, if we don't repeat the story, nothing will change. It is our only hope. Even if it is only a hope.

In her 1964 review of Rolf Hochhuth's play *The Deputy*, about Pope Pius XII's inaction in the face of the Holocaust (reprinted in *Against Interpretation and Other Essays*), Susan Sontag wrote:

> In calling the murder of the six million a tragedy, we acknowl-
> edge that the event is, in some sense, incomprehensible.
> Ultimately, the only response is to continue to hold the event
> in mind, to remember it. This capacity to assume the burden of
> memory is not always practical. Sometimes remembering alle-
> viates grief or guilt; sometimes it makes it worse. Often, it may
> not do any good to remember. But we may feel that it is right,
> or fitting, or proper. This moral function of remembering is
> something that cuts across the different worlds of knowledge,
> action and art.

In such a view there is hope. But since I don't want to appear a roman-tic, I should like a survivor of the Holocaust to bear the last words in this talk. Here is Blanca Rosenberg in her 1993 memoir, *To Tell at Last: Survival Under False Identity, 1941–1945*: "The Nazis were defeated, and the lives we had fought for so very hard were secure at last. But what were they worth? We had no families, no homes, no future—only an unbearable past. As if for the first time, our minds became fully open to the ghetto pictures and smells accumulated over so many years; of unmarked graves; of air rancid with the smell of decomposing bodies."

The talk ended. Senada, who had done the simultaneous transla-tion, was completely exhausted. But the conversation with those in attendance continued, and although I can still see the room and the people, I only remember two things. One is what Claude Lanzmann said, that "it was the most intense discussion" he had ever participated in, and that he was "embarrassed to talk about the Shoah in this room given what these people had to endure and were living with." I could not have agreed more. The other is Suada telling me that those in the room opened up more than she had ever seen before.

At the end of the weekend I didn't want to leave Sarajevo. I wanted to see and hear more. I didn't want to let go of the intensity. I felt an obligation not to turn away from this city, this destruction, these people, even though the guns were now silent. I was beginning to understand something I hadn't understood before about the experiences of the victims and survivors of war and genocide. I began to understand something about the physical presence of threat, the isolation and helplessness, the deep need to recreate some semblance of normal life in the midst of its very destruction. And I knew from my study of the Holocaust that "liberation" was often as difficult for the survivors as the experience of the Holocaust itself. I knew that for the inhabitants of Sarajevo, for the population who had lived or were living in Bosnia-Herzegovina, this postwar period might well be as difficult as the war itself. The only thing I could do was not become a stranger, not forget the stories, not refuse to tell the stories. And so I crossed back over the line, trying not to lose the memory of Sarajevo.

Upon my return to Washington, nothing felt comfortable because everything *was* comfortable: my apartment, its running water, the electricity, the buildings without shell holes, my workplace, the grocery stores, the abundance of trees. Everything was in sharp contrast to Sarajevo, even the conversations I had, which now seemed dull to me. I tried to explain what I had seen, heard, and felt, but I continually came up short.

Before I left for Sarajevo, my good friend Neenah Ellis, who had been there on assignment for National Public Radio, told me, "You will never be the same again." Back home in Washington, I tried to keep myself in Sarajevo, but I couldn't manage it. I tried because I was afraid to forget what I had seen and felt. I wanted to hold on to the immediacy of the sensations I had during my stay there. For a few weeks, I felt out of place in my own life. And then things all went back to normal even as the memory of that time, that place, and those people remained with me, and remain with me still.

When I arrived in Sarajevo in 1996, it all seemed strange yet familiar: familiar because I had read and talked so much about the war and watched so many documentaries about it, but deeply strange because everything, the people and the very geography of the place, made it starkly clear that I had never experienced war or genocide, in Bosnia or anywhere else. More, it forced me to realize something I'd known, but never in such a visceral way: that the history of the Holocaust was both close and distant to me. This all sounds so naïve and obvious to me now, but it's very easy to believe that you understand a situation because you've read or heard so many descriptions of it. It's very easy to forget that the language of these descriptions is not equivalent to the experience itself and gives only an illusory sense of that experience.

My own talk in Sarajevo revealed my ignorance, which lay behind my fear of talking to these people about what they had experienced and I had not. The trip and the talk brought home to me that what seems familiar in a situation is only loosely familiar and that embedded in the situation is a great deal that is unfamiliar or strange. In Sarajevo I encountered head-on my lifelong companions, the strange and the familiar, and came home with them.

SIX

Breast Cancer

When I first began assembling this collection, I thought that my essay on breast cancer would fall somewhere in the middle. I never imagined that I would be placing it at the end. After two mastectomies and two courses of treatment, first in 1993 and then in 2009, I blithely assumed that cancer was done, over.

I was surprised to find, when I read my breast cancer diary from 1993, that I was always worried, consciously or unconsciously, about a recurrence or about developing some other kind of cancer. Apparently I didn't want to be one of those people who always concluded when something physical was amiss that it must be cancer. I systematically denied my own concerns. I did not want to believe that cancer was always in remission and never cured. I simply did not want to be consumed by fear. So it was a big surprise to me, and not a pleasant one, that I was diagnosed with a recurrence of my 2009 breast cancer in 2018.

I wasn't the only one who was surprised. None of my doctors thought I had cancer. No one did, except for my lymphedema therapist, Maureen McBeth. "I don't know what's happening here. I've never seen this before," said my oncologist, Dr. Fred Smith, after he read an MRI report from September 2018 and advised me to see a radiation oncologist. I had never heard him speak this way before, nor had his head nurse, who had been with him for decades. I was grateful for his honesty, but his bewilderment made me nervous, since he had been treating breast cancer for more than thirty years. Why was my condition such a mystery?

I have had some lymphedema since 2009 or 2010, but until 2017 I did not experience an enlargement of my right arm or the fact of having much less movement on my right side than on my left. It's another surprising development for me. I guess I thought that once I had undergone all the recommended therapies I could simply go on with my life as if nothing had happened. Clearly I was mistaken.

My internist, Dr. Lynn Alonso, referred me to a radiation oncologist in Columbia, Maryland, Dr. Sheila Cheston, for an opinion as to whether the mass found on the MRI was typical of radiation fibrosis. Dr. Cheston told me that her instincts and her diagnostic skills suggested that the mass was indeed an effect of radiation and not any sort of cancer recurrence. I was relieved, as was Ellen, my partner of ten years. Although Dr. Cheston was pretty sure it wasn't cancer, she was going to talk with the technologist who did the MRI as well as the oncologist who directed my radiation treatment in 2010. She also decided to send my case to the tumor board for further opinion.

The tumor board did not agree with her. While they didn't declare that the mass they saw on the MRI was cancer, they certainly thought it was suspicious. They wanted me to get a PET scan, and I did, but that scan wasn't definitive either, so I had to have a biopsy. The biopsy *was* definitive: a recurrence of my 2009 breast cancer. After one year of asking questions and having doctors assure me that what they saw was not cancer, we found that it was. Maureen, a lymphedema and cancer rehab specialist with her Master of Physical Therapy degree, had been right all along.

I find it interesting that I never seemed to focus on the possibility of recurrence. Denial can be quite wonderful. But in fact it was always in the back of my mind, and now, unfortunately, it's in the forefront. Since the diagnosis I think about disease and its ramifications almost all the time. I hate it, yet I'm trying to be calm, which is hard to do when I'm awake. I do have moments when I think about it not at all, or else it would paralyze me. How do you think about cancer anyway? Cancer in most of its stages doesn't even feel as serious as a slight cold.

Just as bad as the cancer diagnosis in 2018 is the limited movement of my right hand and arm. It's hard to put on my clothes. I have much less power in my right hand than in my left, so when I try to play the piano with both hands, I can't. I can't write much unless I wear a very restrictive splint—but then my writing isn't what it used to be anyway. Ellen and I have come to call my arm and hand "Flipper." It's difficult to read the paper or a book. Washing dishes or showering is a major undertaking. It's strange to deal with this external manifestation of the cancer inside while trying to be realistic about both.

I was certain that my story of breast cancer was to be about the past, but the treatment I received for the right-side cancer in 2009–10 still affects me in ways I couldn't have imagined. I am really angry about the recurrence and saddened by the prospect of what may come. I am not ready to die or even to be sick, but I find myself thinking about death a lot of the time. I wonder what I should do now—prepare for the end? Well, I'm not going to. My current meds seem to be working, and I'm going to continue as if this is my life now, because it is. The end is a mystery anyway. No one knows when it will come or how.

No matter what we wish, life is framed by birth at one end and death at the other. There is no escape. Our lives reside inside this frame, with all their attendant joys and sorrows, successes and failures. Although we are all going to die, we tend not to dwell on the fact. We just live until faced with death, whether by disease, old age, accident, or any other cause.

When we are healthy, our bodies are our silent companions. We may feel so comfortable that we pay almost no attention to them. A cold, a hangnail, or a sprained ankle may tweak our bodily consciousness because they disrupt everyday life. More serious physical and psychological problems—artery blockage, pulmonary disorders, weight gain, bulimia, anorexia, depression, schizophrenia, cancer—disrupt everyday life dramatically and may soak us in bodily consciousness. I've always had a desire not to be too conscious of my body. I know I carry it, but I would prefer not to be reminded of it with each step. This is in part, I think, why I used to stare at people who could only walk with crutches or could only move in a wheelchair, or whose blindness forced them to walk with a service dog or a cane. I would privately express thanks that I was not in their condition. I attempted to imagine my world without light or easy mobility, but it was almost impossible for me to grasp the effort it took to live in the world without bodily ease. At work one day at the Holocaust Museum, I met a woman who walked with two hand crutches because of a profound problem in her legs. As she left, I watched her walk from the exit door of the museum to her car, which would have taken me no more than thirty seconds, but it took her about ten minutes. It was humbling to imagine what sort of physical and mental stamina that walk required of her. I wondered if she thought about her apparent limitations a lot or if only those of us who walked easily thought about them. It seemed to me that such people must live with a profound consciousness of their own bodies, their every action a reminder of limitation. I have a different view now because of Flipper. It's simple. You have to figure out ways to live with it or not.

I don't mean to say that I have no consciousness of my body. I love nice clothes. I take care of my hair, put on some makeup, on occasion get a pedicure or a manicure. I want my body to be responsive, not recalcitrant, to be pain-free, not pain-ridden. It always feels better to live without having trouble with my body. But what happens when health is disrupted or interrupted? What happens when the interruption has the sound of a possible disaster? What happens when the word "cancer" is used? Being told you have a serious illness forces a consciousness that makes you wary.

My life has been divided: before cancer and after cancer, or perhaps more accurately, before and after chemotherapy and eventually radiation. I travel with a sense of vulnerability. I cannot avoid the unevenness of my body produced by two mastectomies.

What I find most telling is how faulty my memory of the treatments is. I remember some things, mainly tiredness, but other things escape me—neuropathy, mouth sores. I hid the fear from myself, it seems. I focused on other things: my need to be good-humored and more or less calm so people would feel comfortable; my astonishment at the outpouring of help from friends and staff at the Holocaust Museum; my sometime desire to leave my job and disconnect from the Holocaust.

Once you have had breast cancer (perhaps any cancer), it's difficult not to think about it unconsciously or consciously every day. This is especially true if you have had a mastectomy or something equally visible. You see it every day. Every morning I glance at the mirror and notice again that I have no breasts. On some mornings it feels as if I'm seeing this "empty space" for the first time. Often, I don't want to look. It's a psychological discomfort for sure. I once told a doctor that when I look at my chest, it reminds me of my father. I was not terribly interested in or comfortable looking at my body even when I was younger and more attractive, but this absence of breasts seems to mean something. What? Lack of normalcy? Cancer is present in spite of my various forms of denial.

After my first mastectomy, which removed my left breast, I walked around without a bra or prosthesis for the first couple of months. Given the wound, there was no alternative. I noticed that people were staring at my chest, but I didn't care. The most serious stares came from people who knew I'd had the operation, as if they were searching for its effects. Later, when I'd come home from work and change into a T-shirt and jeans, I didn't like the look of my body without the prosthesis. I often kept it on until I went to bed, especially when I had guests in the apartment. Perhaps if my lingering breast had been small it wouldn't have mattered to me so much. Then I'd have had a flat chest with a small rise on the right. Instead what I had was a rather large mound on the right side with a depression on the left side. Once I got the prosthesis, the look of evenness mattered to me a lot. I rarely went without it.

After all this time, I find it hard to define exactly what my discomfort was all about. It's easy to think that there was a great deal I didn't process about this first experience of cancer. Perhaps the missing breast—the long-gone breast—was a constant reminder of what I wished had not happened. It certainly seems that I should have adjusted sooner, but the reminder caught me daily no matter what. What did it bring back? The actual experience? The meaning of the experience? The fear that it might happen again? Fifteen years later, it did happen again, in my right breast.

On June 1, 1993, about two months after the opening of the United States Holocaust Memorial Museum, I went to my internist, Dr. James Ramey, for a routine checkup. He felt a suspicious lump in my breast and made an appointment for me with one of the best breast cancer surgeons in DC, Dr. Kathy Alley. I saw her the next day. She examined me and said she thought the lump was cancer but she would have to do a biopsy to be sure. The biopsy was on Friday, June 4.

The morning before the biopsy I took a shower, and I remember seeing red water coursing down my body to the drain. I also remember wishing that the diagnosis would be cancer. To this day, I have no idea what that red water was all about. Perhaps I was seeing some kind of vulnerability or visualizing blood leaving my body? I also have no idea why I hoped for cancer. Somehow I wanted the diagnosis to be cancer, as if this were something I had to go through. I have always found my thought process perplexing, even shaming. I still wonder what the hell I was thinking. What the hell was I playing with when I said to myself that I wanted to have cancer? What motivated me? An unconscious need for attention or help? Punishment for something I did or was? Did it have something to do with the Holocaust survivors I'd been interviewing? Did I need some harsh experience? Did I want the trauma? Many years later, when I was well into a wonderful relationship with Ellen, who was a therapist, we went to a party together. Another therapist there asked if I suffered from PTSD because of all my interviews with survivors. I vehemently said no, but now I'm not so sure.

In any case, I got my wish. Dr. Alley did the biopsy and told me we were dealing with two different cancers in the breast. I would have to wait for the full biopsy report, but I had no doubt that this wasn't a bright picture. That night some friends came over with pizza, and we had a strangely riotous evening in my apartment. The next day, on Saturday, Dr. Alley called to tell me I had to have a mastectomy. "Fuck," I said. I have no idea what she thought about my saying the f-word or if she even heard it. We made an appointment to talk about the operation on Monday, June 7.

The National Zoo was across the street from my apartment building, and I took a walk there after Dr. Alley's call. Back home, I wrote about it in my diary: "I walked alone in the zoo today late in the afternoon and saw the baby giraffe and gorillas. On the way I had a strange thought—killing my beast, knifing it. Bloody and violent thoughts." My mind had slipped into writing "beast" instead of "breast," but perhaps my mind had it right.

The days following the discovery of the lump and the reality of cancer produced a flurry of phone calls and conversations. I could not stop talking. My calls spread across the country to friends and then to friends of friends who had had breast cancer. I went to a bookstore, bought a few books on breast cancer, and read them when I wasn't talking on the phone. Life became heightened. I had a clear purpose, if a narrow one, as I focused on the cancer and how to beat it. Not much got in the way. I didn't let little things bother me. I had no time for the trivial. I had no strength for the tedious or even the dramatic issues at the museum that would have engaged my energies before. I had a cat, Foxy, whose condition of amyloidosis was exacerbated by my behavior and my illness. I was not able to pay sufficient attention to him, and I suspect he was affected by all the tension surrounding my condition. He eventually became so ill that I had to put him down.

As it happened, my dad was in town on vacation at the time of my diagnosis and was staying with my brother, Ted. When I told them both about the diagnosis, they were stunned. I felt I couldn't discuss my diagnosis with either of them because they would simplty tell me to rely on the doctors and do whatever they said, or perhaps I could not bear how much the diagnosis upset them. It wasn't as if we could have a conversation about alternatives, and I seemed to have no alternatives anyway, except to do nothing or go ahead with a mastectomy and chemo. Nothing I'd read suggested otherwise. No one I'd talked with suggested otherwise. My one thought was to try acupuncture alongside the other treatment I had to have. My father eventually told me he would pay for wigs, acupuncture, and anything else I might need.

The operation was to be on June 11. The night before, I decided that I wanted to take a picture of my breasts. I wanted to have more than a memory of two breasts. What has always seemed ironic to me is that the picture came out completely black—no breasts were to be seen. Apparently, when I took the picture, my camera was in the way. If I'd had an iPhone, I could have taken a breast selfie. Now I only have my memory of two breasts and the memory of trying to get a picture.

Sometimes I wonder how I got through the operation and the months of chemo. I tended to be good-humored, and my cheerfulness made others comfortable. If I ever expressed alarm, most people simply wanted the alarm to vanish. Friends were frightened. Some told me that they went to a therapist to talk about it. One person told me that she prayed for me every Sunday in church. Many people from the Holocaust Museum donated money for cancer research. I got more attention than I can ever remember getting in my life. Cancer was not a familiar occurrence to many at the museum, and I suspect this had something to do with all the attention. There was also a great deal of love that came my way, for which I have been always grateful. I sent out an email to thank people for the flowers, cards, well wishes, smiles, hugs, and concern. I said, "While I may be uneven in some respects, your support helps me to remain sort of even emotionally. . . . This has been enough excitement for a while [and has] taught me again that life is not to be described as filled with stability—the constant is change and surprise, it seems." One answer I received from a colleague is a prime example of the way people gave me so much, sometimes too much: "Even the glib Communications Director doesn't have words to express her admiration for your bravery, your attitude—maybe even panache? I hope if I ever have to face a situation like you have, I do it with half the courage. In the midst of all this professional shit, you are a sterling reminder of what is really important. Thank you."

I was actually more afraid of the chemo than the cancer. Cancer felt remote, a distant diagnosis with no apparent consequences, in that I had no symptoms, no pain, no discomfort at all. But there was nothing remote about the experience of chemotherapy. It was the cure, or at least some way to fight the cancer, but it affected me a great deal. This was how it seemed to me, but I now suspect that it was all very much more complicated. Then again, maybe not.

During my course of treatment, I mostly didn't play the piano or even read a book or long articles. Chemotherapy seemed to preclude two of the most important and relieving activities in my life. I hated this new fact of life, but I had no choice, and it taught me how much energy and concentration it takes to focus on words that become ideas or stories, or on notes that become themes or musical ideas. When you have cancer, you have to rely on something else: loving friends and family who don't mind your exhaustion or your inability to remember, people who have patience and can listen, and people who have hope. What did it mean to have cancer? Anything? Everything? When you have cancer, life is refocused and narrowed, yet at the same time widened.

My dear friend Alex Zapruder, with whom I spent a riotous day when she and I went shopping for a wig or two, once told me that I had a "presentation self"—namely, what I presented in public and what was expected of me—and that it must be exhausting for me to keep it up. She also said that I was more tired for the eight or so months following chemotherapy than I seemed to be when I was on chemo. I remember thinking that at least I had a good reason to be tired during chemo but how boring it was to have no sign of disease except my fuzzy hair growing in and still be exhausted all the time, even after ten or fifteen hours of sleep.

I kept a diary in the months after my first mastectomy, and I include excerpts here as perhaps the truest reflection of what I was experiencing, though I have added some bracketed comments from my present vantage point, or occasionally for clarification.

Wednesday, June 9, 1993

No reconstruction. Couldn't do it given Alley's schedule. . . . Felt relieved. . . . I really didn't want to go through the strain of such a long operation even if it was feasible. . . . But . . . reconstruction wasn't possible because of [my] hysterectomy. . . .

I couldn't [use my] stomach muscles [in the operation] ... and would have to get skin and muscle from my back. This would lengthen the surgery by about 10 hours and I was not about to do that.

Friday, June 11, 1993 [day of operation]

Dr. Alley arrived [at the hospital] about 8 a.m. She was beautiful and warm. I asked her not to forget which breast should be removed and that I had a plane to catch to Paris and could she make sure I could make it. She said yes. What was I doing? ... impossible for me to get my feelings out or afraid if I did it would be bad for me?

In the recovery room my head and speech seemed separated from my body. I asked some questions but only remember some foggy feeling. Post recovery was quite a sight—Dad, Ted, Raye, Shana, Alex, Karen and Aleisa. Smiles, kisses, handholding. I remember that Dad was on the bed next to mine and I think that Alex was on his side, perhaps holding his hand, and Ted was nearby. Flowers arrived [from whom I don't know]. Elaine and Marjorie came later that evening. David and Kevin called. I talked a lot on the phone on Friday night after surgery. I wore myself down. Visitors galore. Even Theresa Wobbe and Gudrun Schwarz were in from [Germany and attended] the Berkshire Conference on the History of Women, where I was supposed to participate on a panel. [They read my paper at the conference.]

Sunday, June 13, 2:45 a.m. [written in the hospital]

[I am remembering my] last day at the office before the operation—many different emotions. Some people too shy to talk but ask how I am; others just smile and wish me well; still others visibly upset and shaken it seems. Some of the latter group too difficult for me. I don't want to see fear. I think I probably don't want it to connect to my own fear and that would double it.

Shaike Weinberg, the founding director of the Holocaust Museum came to see me in my office. We hug and sit knee to knee in my little, messy office. He asks about the operation and my spirit. He wants me to fight. We both sort of cry or just have some rolling tears in our eyes. I told him I loved him and he said he loved me.

Sunday, June 20

What goes through my mind—a sort of disbelief about what has happened and what I must figure out, understand and decide. I think it will take much energy and support. Am I afraid? Sometimes. Do I fear dying? No. But I don't want to die. And I don't think this is a death sentence. I think my chances are good that I will get through and over this. I will be cured. But this is complex.

And one of the most complex parts is all the people relating to me. And how we are relating. So much contact and no time or need to be depressed. Am I angry? Am I in the middle of a drama? Somehow I feel focused and centered. And while this is nothing I want, this breast cancer is what I must live with and figure out how to defeat. Does it feel like a battle? Yes and no. In some way—not quite a battle—but cure IS what I have as the goal. The battle is not my body—but this invader—ah so it is a battle yet I don't feel embattled. [How could I have called cancer an invader when I knew it came from inside my own body?] I feel in control. How can this be? Why is there more calm? Is it because I am not alone? Is it because so much love and affection moves towards me? So much touching, concern, smiles, laughter, sadness even—Surgery was not unknown to me—chemo is a mystery—I am apprehensive and wonder what it will do to my body beyond killing cancer cells. Will it harm me? How? How defeat the harm? I don't feel frayed. I feel centered and able to deal and continually to say "raus, raus." [I am so not frayed now as not to notice that the word I used here was a word I'd heard from survivors who told me that it was what the Nazis said during deportations and when people got off the trains at killing centers: "Raus, raus!" Was this a slip or what? Sometimes, in rereading these entries, I almost can't believe what I wrote.]

June 25 [first meeting with my oncologist.]

Dr. Smith was in an old-fashioned brick building that felt extremely comfortable. When Dr. Smith walked into the office—I liked his face and hands. He said that he knew about my case but wanted to know how I found out about the cancer and what I felt, had I assimilated the information—this is what I think he asked. It was just right. Nothing patronizing just eyes looking directly at me and interested in what I had to say. I think I was flabbergasted. [My good friend Dr. Sally Rudicel, who was a student of mine at DePauw and now was a bone surgeon, came with me to Dr. Smith's office because she thought that her medical expertise might be helpful. Aside from answering a few questions she asked, Dr. Smith did not even look at her. He only paid attention to me.]

We talked about the protocol—CAF—the stronger of the regimens for this kind of cancer. He explained why. [CAF, standing for Cytoxan, Adriamycin, and Fluorouracil, was used to treat cancers with a high likelihood of recurrence and was much harder on the body than the alternative, CMF, Cytoxin, Methetrexate, and Fluorouracil.] I probably blanched at the thought. He kept saying "we will help you through this" and I believed him. I felt safe somehow. (It was from July to Dec. every three weeks.) Smith said that I was recovering fine and that I didn't look as if I had had an operation a little over a week ago. [Actually, it was two weeks ago.]

June 29, 1993

I am feeling tired and a little undermined. Today when I talked with Art Levine (Ruth Levine's husband) he began to say "when you don't think you can vomit anymore just remember the treatment is helping" or some such phrase—and I swear my stomach turned and I felt nauseous. Are we all so damned suggestible? What is this chemotherapy myth anyway? But why the hell would he talk in such a crude way about this? This is what I don't understand now. Who knew how much the chemo would or could affect me? But perhaps it was a bit of a reality that I wasn't facing?

. . . I want more energy. I feel tired but I am having trouble resting or napping. Concentration is not up to par. Hah! That is an understatement. . . . Am I becoming angry or what? Annoyed? Too tired somehow?

I am finally afraid and sad. [It is strange that I remember none of this. At least I said it somewhere—I don't think I said it to many people, if at all.]

July 3, 1993

After seeing Fred Smith I go to Catch Can [on Connecticut

Avenue in DC] and buy $400 worth of clothes. What is happening? Somehow I don't want to refuse myself. Something has been liberated to look well, to have fun and to laugh.

July 8, 1993

I wore the longish dark wig my first day back [at work]. Almost no one recognized me and when they realized who it was I kept getting compliments that I looked 10 years younger. The men at the office found the wig quite sexy—how strange. On the other hand, some women were uncomfortable—how odd.

So much is different—last weekend seemed to lose my center and there is terror in me sort of—will this cancer overtake me at some time—5 [years], 10? 20? I generally feel centered and ready to keep fighting with the only thing I have—my spirit, my humor, and resourcefulness.

August 15 [excerpts from a letter to Dr. Smith]

I thought I would write you a few lines . . . so you will know what I have been thinking and feeling prior to the next chemo appointment.

. . . this past Thursday I seem to feel more vulnerable and more frightened and more unsure than at any another time since the diagnosis of breast cancer. Perhaps getting mouth sores was the last straw. Or realizing that there is some effect on my eyes that I cannot read as much as usual and that my eyes tear and don't feel very comfortable. Or perhaps it was about time that I was able to feel this vulnerable. I began to get angry at chemotherapy and wondered whether you could show me the studies that would indicate that I am not abusing my body now, not just temporarily staving off cancer—but that there is good reason to believe that this can really do some long-term good.

I began to feel as if I was in a crapshoot. That there is no real protection or rather no sure protection. And of course there is no such protection in life—I know that. But I need something more tangible that will indicate that this type of cancer that I had/have and the DNA analysis that is mine can be treated with some degree of success. I spoke with Dr. Alley [and] she assured me that this is so. She was of course very supportive. But I need to know from you.

I know that I won't stop chemo, but I must say that it was in my thoughts this week a good deal. The sapping of energy, the feeling of not being too well even when I feel better is no easy thing. It isn't the myths about chemo that need to be discussed. . . . It isn't the extremes that are so difficult. It is the incremental assault that adds up to a difficult time. . . .

I don't know if you can allay some of my fears or my anger—perhaps for me finally getting some of them out of my system helped to relieve the tension about them. I have not called on you or Dr. Alley and I think I will now feel freer to express the kinds of thoughts I have and ask for some help. . . .

I've been dealing with this in as practical and good humored away as I know how. It seemed that I could not allow myself to stop and think too much even though I read a good deal about breast cancer and chemotherapy. To focus too much on me meant I couldn't make a lot of the decisions that I had to make and make quickly. Now there are few decisions—only vigilance and constant care so that I can keep as healthy as possible—and so perhaps I am able to reflect or allow my reflections to become more conscious to myself. The process is quite fascinating although I barely understand it. I have no real idea of what it means to have cancer. It still seems unreal in some ways.

But the affect and effect of having cancer and the ways in which we deal with it surely [are] becoming familiar. Perhaps that is the way we deal with disease.

[I was sure I had written that I would never do this chemo again, but there is nothing to that effect in the letter. I think I must have said it to Dr. Smith during an appointment and he answered that I shouldn't be so sure. He indicated that there might be a vaccine and one would not have to go through chemotherapy. I think we did have this conversation, but I have no record of it.]

September 1993, Labor Day

A colleague asked me what were my biggest concerns given what is happening. I couldn't really answer: what is it? fear, anticipation, tiredness, inability to think well; relationships? what did I say. I can't even remember what I tried to communicate to her. One of the things that I think I said was that I wanted to have a life beyond work. And in fact now I think that is something I am doing. This work is not that satisfying except when I am interviewing or working on a program.

Ramey [my internist] asked me if I was sad. What an interesting question. Am I sad? I told someone that I seemed to be o.k. most of the time. Unless I was constantly giving myself lies ...

October 8, 1993

Did do laundry. Not eating enough veggies that is for sure and I need to eat more lettuce. Do I need more help with my food intake. Someone to cook for me? More company perhaps. I think my being alone this week was no good. But what can

I do about this? should I plan to be with people more? get menus and buy out more? At least now I can order food from the food delivery service.

This is so boring—how the hell is this going to help. Oy I must believe it will but the only thing I seem to think about is how to get through this daily existence. Although remember Joan that you are reading more and certainly your work is not suffering very much. If I can get through that box of interviews it would be great. So I will try to do that as well this weekend and the performance thing—what is it for heavens sake that I am supposed to write? Can I even figure it out?

January 12, 1994

Does cancer change your life? Do I have to have new values? no—I think that I simply need to take more relaxing time—more vacation—more fun— How the hell does one find time to do what one wants in life—no way. Books, movies, music, playing piano, walking, traveling. . . .

Why don't I go to bed earlier even though I am tired. Something keeps me wanting to stay awake. Perhaps it is because I don't come home relaxed.

Perhaps it was because I was afraid I wouldn't wake up. I recently came across some notes I made in 2000, when I was trying to write about my experience with breast cancer. One of them reads, "I have to say this writing is disturbing me. I am feeling rough on the inside. As if I am scraping my body in order to write about this. It surprises me that after seven years, trying to talk about it seems to hurt in some physical way. What is it? A kind of superstition? What am I afraid of in going there?"

At the end of treatment in 1994, I bought two Abyssinian kittens, Isaac and Willy, from Foxy's breeder. Because of his amyloidosis she hadn't been able to adopt him out before I came along, so she was more than pleased to offer me two of her kittens. They were terrific to have around me. Isaac had to be put down in 2008 because of kidney disease, and Willy was put down in 2010. Those decisions were hard.

When I was diagnosed with cancer in my right breast in 2009, I went back to my old surgeon, Dr. Kathy Alley. After examining me, she was convinced from what she saw on the biopsy (done by the radiologist at the mammography clinic I went to) that I would not need chemotherapy or radiation. How wrong she was. During the operation, she removed seventeen positive lymph nodes, which meant that I would clearly have to have chemo and probably radiation too, not to mention another mastectomy.

Life was different for me then. I'd retired from the museum in 2007 and had been with Ellen for a year. During my previous bout with cancer, I'd been showered with care, but nothing could match having someone as close as Ellen in my life. She had lost her partner of twenty years to ovarian cancer in 1999, so the fact that I now had cancer presented her with many difficulties. She uneasily told me that she couldn't attend my chemo treatments because it was simply too much to go through again. I understood and I knew I would miss her, but I decided to schedule my chemo treatments on days when she was seeing her therapy patients so there would be no apparent conflict. She recently revealed to me that she was terrified I would leave her because she couldn't come to chemo. I never had that inclination. I too was terrified that she would leave me because of the cancer, and I too said nothing. Each of us was trying to protect the other by not really talking about our feelings.

At the time Ellen lived in Columbia, Maryland, and I was in DC. She was allergic to cats, so I drove to see her every weekend. I have no idea where I got the physical strength to do that when I'd been feeling so exhausted all week, but somehow I did, and it made all the difference in the world to have one person focusing on me when I needed it most. I knew how difficult it was for her, and I appreciate what she did for me more than she'll ever know.

In DC, my dear friend Sarah Ogilvie from the Holocaust Museum organized people to provide me with dinners, drive me to and from chemo treatments, and drive me to get a booster shot the day after chemo. It was an incredible operation, and this attention was something I needed more than I knew. I cannot thank Sarah enough. I only wish that I'd spent time with more people than I did. I was convinced that I was too tired to socialize or carry on a conversation. What I didn't realize until very late was that seeing people was energizing rather than debilitating.

I didn't keep a diary during that time, but I did start a blog to update concerned friends on what was going on with me. "This is a difficult time for me," I wrote in my first post, on October 26, 2009, "but I want you to know that my communication with you and you with me is about as essential as any therapy I can get." Some excerpts from subsequent posts follow, again with bracketed comments.

Third Post
October 28, 2009

As some of you know, I used to teach philosophy. Certain of my intro classes had a lot of stuff about the relationship between life and death. I quoted Plato ("Philosophy is learning how to die."); or Socrates through Plato ("The unexamined life is not worth living."); or Heidegger ("As soon as man comes to life, he is at once old enough to die."); or Kierkegaard ("The unlived life is not worth examining."); or Tolstoy in the short story "The Death of Ivan Ilyich" (something like "What if I have lived my life all wrong?") .... The list went on and on.

What has seemed true in recent years is that I had no idea what I was talking about when I began to teach. One can easily ponder the serious questions about the relationship between life and death as metaphors. Until one confronts its inevitability either through illness or age itself, there is something about death that does not—to many of us—seem real. There are things that change that for too many people around the world: war, oppression, random killings, genocide, etc. Some of us, fortunately or not, remain strangers to this all too inevitable ending of what we call our lives. Perhaps we are always strangers to our own demise.

Enough on this.

Fourth Post
October 29, 2009

The good news: the PET SCAN showed no cancer anywhere. This means that I will probably have to do chemo and radiation. However, as there is no spread of the cancer, its complexities seem less than it appeared to be a few days ago.

What was interesting to me (as I drove to my surgeon's office to get some draining done on the incision) was that I was completely focused on my body and its vulnerabilities. I began to wonder what I should sell or give away to make things easier for people if there was a spread of cancer and I would die soon.

I had an internal terror that did not feel familiar to me. I think that I find death wrong even if intellectually I know that living forever could be a curse. I also know that there is no right time to die for anyone—or so it appears—but it really seemed to be the wrong time for me now even though I am hardly young anymore. One becomes very ego driven in these circumstances.

I couldn't eat much, or listen to music, or play the piano. A little TV baseball was about my speed. It has been a revealing few days. I am not sure I can keep the tension alive that was produced by fearing I would soon die of cancer—any more than I could keep the bombed out areas I saw in 1996 Sarajevo alive for very long. And yet, there is something about that tension, about that fear that may well be helpful to keep conscious.

Enough for now. . . I will probably go out to get a steak to beef up (so to speak) my red cells . . . or something.

Thank you all for your concern and care.

Fifth Post
November 2, 2009

. . . I no longer feel as if my life could end quickly—but I know that this is a complex disease and cannot be experienced as one might experience a broken arm. The desire for science in these matters is really a myth—treatment is an art or a crap shoot—or perhaps both at once.

More later. . . .

Sixth Post
November 9, 2009

I am finding the waiting problematic. My surgeon wants the oncologist to start chemo and the oncologist seems to want to wait until the surgeon finishes draining the wound. [This, as well as problems with installing a port for administering the chemo drugs, was the cause of many subsequent delays in my treatment.] I am calling everyone to make certain that no one—especially me—is waiting longer than necessary. I would just like this part to start so I can get it over with and then radiation will come soon enough.

The truth is, I would rather just run away from all this but that is not in the cards it seems.

Ninth Post
November 15, 2009

. . . Waiting makes some of us crazy and plans not being what they were supposed to be drives others of us crazy. Sometimes it is both things that make one want to scream something or other to someone or other. Perhaps it is simply having a disease over which control may seem possible, may feel possible but is a mirage. Yet control we want to have. There has to be a future beyond the treatments and the worry. At least one must hope.

12th Post
November 24, 2009

It appears that next Tuesday, December 1, 2009, will be my first chemo treatment.

It is somehow more unnerving to me than it was years ago. This may be because I had to wait and not know when it would be; or it might be because I am older and know more; or it might be that the second time around does not feel better. It is hard to know what causes anxiety. Whatever the cause, there will be no getting around it next week and then it will go on for 6 sessions at 3 week intervals. One way or the other I will be ready . . . but a little unwilling I suspect. . . .

13th Post
December 1, 2009

Well, this was the day I waited for and dreaded. My first chemo treatment. It was not so bad but there was a lot of information to take in—concerns about side effects and side effects and more side effects. Nothing about front effects though....

14th Post
December 7, 2009

... I have to admit that the extreme tiredness from the chemo is completely unpleasant. They say that the only thing that might help is some exercise—so I push myself in spite of it all seeming to be counterintuitive. Perhaps over time it will be helpful. I will go to a personal trainer this week and see what he can do ... who knows.

I try to keep up my spirits but they seem a bit deflated so I will go tomorrow and get some blood tests to see if my white cells are too low.

I would like to write about other things—e.g., Tiger Woods and his escapades ... but I have to admit that my small world of chemo seems to take over even though I want it to be otherwise. Perhaps some distractions will help. I find that listening to music is more distracting than the TV um ...

15th Post
December 13, 2009

... I said in an earlier post that music was distracting for me and TV wasn't. What I mean is that listening to music felt soothing [hence distracting] and TV seemed to rattle me more.

I can even play piano some but not as much as I would wish. One friend suggested playing popular music rather than only the classical music I have been playing. It was a really good idea as it is easier and quite relaxing to me. And who knows I might elevate my spontaneity in playing so I don't have to depend upon the written notes quite as much as I have in the past.

Thank you all for your phone calls and notes.

18th Post
December 22, 2009

...There are times when I wish to just run away and not do this anymore. But then I don't run except in my little fantasy world. When I feel good I think I make believe that I am not doing chemo, that I don't have cancer concerns ... and it works until I know that another treatment is coming. Then it all floods back and feels a bit nightmarish—that is, can this really be happening? And then, of course, I wake up to a reality I wish was gone....

19th Post
December 23, 2009

Well, so far so good. I suspect that it is too soon to know much of how this is going to go this time.

Have a conundrum that is a result of my last chemo adventure of 15 years ago. At that point I had no port so they had to put the "cocktail" in my veins. When the first chemo treatment was over and they had me raise my arm to hold onto the cotton ball protecting me from bleeding, I somehow came out with "Heil Hitler." I had never said such a thing in my life and although I worked at the US Holocaust Memorial Museum, it is hardly anything I had thought of saying ever. But somehow the position of my arm and all and some sinister thoughts I suspect, made me do it. Three friends were with me—two of whom worked at the Museum—and they all fell off their chairs laughing. (I have to admit that I was probably a little drunk from the Zofran that they put into the "Cocktail.") One does become somewhat superstitious so I said the same thing one or two more times. Then I had second thoughts because I didn't think that this was a good thing to say. I then said "Fuck Hitler" which felt better and still received some laughs.

Now it seems different. First of all "fuck" seems too good a thing to say and more important, I am stymied because I have a port and there seems to be no opportunity for me to say something. I am perhaps more shy since the room is bigger or I have just forgotten it altogether until I leave.

Perhaps someone has an idea—"Fuck cancer"? but is there not a better phrase. Any ideas would be appreciated. Or perhaps silence is the best medicine?

20th Post
December 30, 2009

It seems that the chemo begins to make me feel like a wet noodle, sometimes a drenched noodle on Friday following the Tuesday chemo and then I am out of it—physically and sometimes mentally—until perhaps the following Wednesday. Then I seem to perk up some and become sort of normal again. The noodleness produced uncomfortable fatigue—so much so that I sometimes cannot stand for too long—and I can do almost nothing except try and rest and watch good or bad movies on the TV. Sometimes I force myself to do things but my spirit does not follow me much. . . . I remain rather hidden in the chemicals—or so it appears.

It feels today (Wed) that I am beginning to come out of the haunt of the chemicals and perhaps will be myself—whatever that means—until the next time. What seems clear is that fighting the tired effects of the chemo does not work—I need to try and be more relaxed about its inevitability no matter how resistant my inner self.

21ˢᵗ Post
January 10, 2010

Back again having felt sort of normal for a little more than a week. And now, of course, I am somewhat apprehensive about the next chemo treatment—it will be the 3rd one and hence means I will be half way through.

But I wonder—why does my heart seem to race too much when I do something like an aerobic workout? Is my hair, thin as it is, actually growing out some and looking funny? why does my wig (which looks similar to my old hairdo) feel strange and out of place even when it is in place (for those who have seen the wig rise out of proportion to its initial placement, you will know what I mean)?; why shouldn't I get the HINI flu shot?; and of course THE QUESTION: why cancer now when life seems better than it has seemed in many years?

Questions also abound about this treatment no matter how much one is told that it will stave off the movement of the cancer cells. It is impossible to really mean that the treatment is worse than the alternative, but it sometimes feels like it.

I have been doing some exercises, even going to a personal trainer every couple of weeks. Does it help? who knows? they say it does. And certainly it doesn't feel worse. And movement is a good thing.

And then there is acupuncture—that does help—for the moment anyway.

And so it goes. Not very interesting. Actually more of the same old, same old with respect to chemo . . . tired, tired and more tired. But I think—even though I suspect that my memory fails me—this time is not as difficult as the chemo I did 15 years ago.

27th Post
February 23, 2010

As they told me today, this was the penultimate treatment. Just one more to go. I am feeling a little bit zonked so I am watching parts of the Olympics and other parts of American Idol. It works for the zonked out.

Only one more chemo treatment to go and then there is a bit of a respite—perhaps 3-4 weeks and on to radiation. While not looking forward to radiation I am hoping that it doesn't take quite so much out of me as the chemo. I guess I will see and hopefully watch the hair grow back and hope for some so-called normalcy. . . .

28th Post
March 2, 2010

Well, there isn't really that much to say except the person who told me this would be a walk in the park in comparison with getting Adriaimycin years ago, was full of it. [Adriamycin was the A in the CFA chemo I received after my first mastectomy.] This new cocktail simply takes the stuffing out of dolls let alone people. I find the exhaustion that rivets me to couches and walls not at all to my liking. Taste buds don't work for days, so practically no food or drink pleases. My edema which seems to be getting better was a surprise. The neuropathy and nail fungus like stuff is a pain. This is not the way one wishes to take on cancer or anything else. I always thought that chemo seemed worse than the disease it is meant to cure . . . but that can't really be the case can it?

Well, I am not looking forward to the last treatment but I am because it means it seems to mean that chemo is over. And I have to say "Hooray" to that.

and the Spring begins to sneak through the wind and bits of snow and that is good news. . . .

31st Post
March 27, 2010

Well, I had my last chemo on March 16 and I just now am beginning to feel like myself—sort of. . . . The eyes still water and my finger nails look horrendous from whatever the chemo brings but I think my hair is slowly returning not to normal but to a growing state. And the lymphedema remains and I am hopeful once the chemo is out of me that the radiation will not make havoc with my body and perhaps this will go away.

Radiation begins on April 19 and on April 1, I take a CT scan to make sure everything has remained clean or something like that.

Once radiation begins I will be back with more news from

Lake Cancer Begone....

35th Post
May 28, 2010

Well, I have 4 more days of radiation to endure. It is not so bad. However, my chest is as red as a lobster and parts of it itch although I am not to touch it so I try hard not to. I put on cortisone cream and miaderm and try to forget it. Most times it works. The treatments have been much easier for me than the chemo. I don't even seem to get too tired at all. I have more energy than I have had in months. It has become difficult for me to simply relax and that I find an odd and somewhat disturbing turn of events. I think the slowing down that chemo creates is not the worst part of it at all.

After next Friday the major treatments will be over and I wonder if I feel bereft.... what is it to just wait....?

I sometimes wonder about progress when it comes to this thing called breast cancer. Although I know there have been some advancements in the years since I had this last in 1993—there are different sorts of diagnoses and perhaps some different sorts of chemo treatments, but for me, it seems oddly similar to years ago. Granted there were more meds to take including a booster the day after chemo, but still it all felt very reminiscent of years ago when I didn't have to do radiation. Now that I have done radiation, it seems that it is more direct or focused than is chemo.... Don't know if I am correct and perhaps cancer is simply too complicated to have made medical progress in 15 years. yet, yet ...

Now I come to the end of the treatments and I don't know about the blog,,,,I may continue just to see what happens and let you all know as I proceed with the clinical trial of a bisphosphonate and start with an aromatase inhibitor. . . . we will see . . .

36ᵗʰ Post
June 14, 2010

The radiation is completed and I am now adjusting to the redness and the itching recede. I cream up and the redness seems to go away little by little.

Now comes a difficult piece I think—waiting. I will take the aromatase inhibitor which is supposed to offer some protection from a return of the cancer—that is supposed to go for 5 years. How often I have to get a PET or a CT scan I am not sure.

It pleases me that the treatments are done—altho I have to admit that radiation was much less than I thought it might be and chemo was worse than radiation by far.

Life appears to be getting back to sort of normal and that feels good. But of course one never knows what will be around the corner. I will continue to write here but it will be less frequent I suspect and perhaps more logical—although this post seems to go all over the place. Sorry about that.

I was convinced when my first course of treatment was completed in 2010 that I could essentially forget cancer, which I mostly did until I was diagnosed with a recurrence of the 2009 cancer in 2018. When I was told that the biopsy showed I had stage 4 cancer, I was convinced that I would die in two or three weeks—hardly time to get things in order, but I tried. I did not succeed. I was also told that there were treatments available. There would be no cure—as if there ever were a cure—but I could live a long time if I responded well to medication.

After discussions with Ellen—by then we were living together in our condo in Columbia, Maryland—I decided to sever my relationship with Dr. Smith. It felt ridiculous to drive all the way to DC for my treatments when I could find another oncologist in Columbia. I also came to wonder about continuing with Dr. Smith because I felt he was unable to respond fully to my symptoms. Although I still found it difficult to switch—after all, I had been his patient for both previous cancers—I met with Dr. Edward Lee and was impressed by his humor, directness, and patience. I asked him to call Dr. Smith, who knew me better than Dr. Lee did, and consult with him about the treatment plan. Dr. Lee told me that in their conversation Smith agreed with Lee's plan for my condition. He said that Dr. Smith would call me, but there was no call. I have no idea what else they may have discussed.

Dr. Lee prescribed Ibrance and letrozole. The assumption was that I would be taking this combo for the rest of my life, and at first it did some good, but after a year or so it proved to be ineffective. In addition, it had side effects that knocked me out of myself, side effects whose origin eluded me and all around me, as I told Dr. Lee after he decided I should stop taking it. I cried more than I ever had, I was disconsolate and morose, and I was filled with dread. When I awoke each morning, I never felt like myself. I had an enormous feeling of negativity and fright that I couldn't shake, nor did I realize how deep it went or how it was affecting others, not only me. I had agreed to take the drug combo because I knew how serious this recurrence was, but I now understand that Ibrance and letrozole created serious side effects for me that were not described in the literature. When Dr. Lee put me on a new chemo drug, Doxil, I was a different person, one recognizable as my old self.

Ellen and I had talked about marriage many times in the course of our relationship, but it never seemed a necessary structure for us. However, almost immediately after this diagnosis of a recurrence, Ellen proposed and I accepted. We were married on November 8, 2018, by a justice of the peace in the Columbia town hall, with friends in attendance. We had a lovely time, including a wonderful celebratory lunch. I had never wanted to be married, but this decision felt right since we had been together for at least ten years and we were more in love and better at relating than ever before. Still, I wonder why Ellen wanted to marry me when I was diagnosed with stage 4 cancer. I think she was very brave.

I started Doxil in December 2019. Within a few months, when Covid-19 emerged, I almost forgot about the cancer and focused instead on a world gone quiet and strange and dangerous. We went into lockdown on March 17, 2020. I did not go grocery shopping (Ellen shopped for us) until June, and any other shopping I did was online. My outside adventures included going for my infusions, walking with Ellen around a beautiful lake nearby, and coffee with her at a Starbucks window. More recently I got my hair cut. I purchased a new car. Phone calls from my brother come regularly. I have felt locked in, but energetic and spirited.

In the summer of 2019, I sent my editor the six essays which became this book: *Companions: The Strange and the Familiar*. This work became a lifesaver for me. The writing brought me back to playing the piano. Cancer had intruded on my right hand and arm so that I could only play with my left hand, and this limitation had affected my desire to play. Now I am learning Scriabin for the left hand. I am not sure of the connection between my writing and music. Perhaps creativity is one answer?

The essays and the queries of my editor, Joy Johannessen (the Joy of my teaching essay), forced me to reconsider different aspects of my life, especially my connection with the Holocaust. For some time I have eschewed reading about or even thinking much about the Holocaust or my work on women and the Holocaust. When Judith Tydor Baumel-Schwartz asked me to write about the Holocaust in my life for the book *Her Story, My Story?*, I was more than reluctant, but with Judy's generous offer to edit what I had written, my reluctance disappeared. And I believe this work enabled me to begin to write the essays that I have been writing in my imagination for years.

The coronavirus pandemic—as awful as it has been for far too many of us—was not awful for me. It enabled me to think about, remember, and write about parts of my life that I had ignored. It gave me good and deep time with Ellen, with whom I share my life. It provided many moments to think about Jews during the Holocaust, African Americans in the United States over the last four hundred years, and other groups we call "minorities."

As I write now, it's been more than two years since my diagnosis. I'm stable at the moment, but there's no telling how long the moment will last or how the cancer might progress. This is what seems so scary— always, always wondering what may happen. Even if Heidegger was right to say that as soon as we are born we are old enough to die, most of us don't live in that shadow. Perhaps we would lead better lives if we did.

I should correct myself. With the coronavirus pandemic, we all live in the shadow of death now, and many—health workers, essential workers, etc.—are leading exemplary lives of self-sacrifice and service. Ellen and I are not young anymore—she is seventy-three and I am eighty-one—but we do what we can for charities and political movements, and as often as we can, we go for rides and walks and to the beach with Flipper, our personal strange but familiar companion in the world we share with others and their companions: the strange and the familiar.

Bibliography of Works Cited

Albee, Edward. *Who's Afraid of Virginia Woolf?* New York: Atheneum Books, 1962.

Arendt, Hannah. *Between Past and Future.* New York: Viking Press, 1969.

_____. "Home to Roost: A Bicentennial Address." *New York Review of Books*, June 26, 1975.

_____. *Men in Dark Times.* New York: Harcourt, Brace & World, 1968.

_____. *Thinking Without a Banister: Essays in Understanding, 1953-1975.* New York: Schocken Books, 2018.

Atkinson, Ti-Grace. *Amazon Odyssey.* Links Books, 1974.

Barbour, Floyd B. *The Black Power Revolt.* Manchester, NH: Extending Horizons Books, 1968.

Baumel-Schwartz, Judith Tydor, and Dalia Ofer, eds. *Her Story, My Story? Writing About Women and the Holocaust.* Bern and New York: Peter Lang, 2020.

Boder, David P. *I Did Not Interview the Dead.* Champaign: University of Illinois Press, 1949.

Buñuel, Luis. *My Last Breath.* London: Virgin Books, 1983.

Burris, Barbara. "The Fourth World Manifesto." In *Radical Feminism,* edited by Anne Koedt, Ellen Levine, and Anita Rapone. New York: Times Books, 1973.

Carmichael, Stokely, and Charles V. Hamilton. *Black Power: The Politics of Liberation in America.* New York: Random House, 1967.

Cernyak-Spatz, Susan. *Protective Custody: Prisoner 34042.* Cortland, NY: N & S Publishers, 2005.

Delbo, Charlotte. *Auschwitz and After* (trilogy), trans. Rosette C. Lamont. 2nd ed. New Haven: Yale University Press, 2014. Includes *None of Us Will Return,* 1965; *Useless Knowledge,* 1970; and *The Measure of Our Days,* 1985.

_____. *Days and Memory,* trans. Rosette Lamont. Marlboro, VT: Marlboro Press, 2001.

Ellison, Ralph. *Invisible Man.* New York: Random House, 1952.

Fast, Howard. *Freedom Road.* Reprint ed. Abingdon, UK: Routledge, 2015.

Faulkner, William. *Requiem for a Nun.* New York: Random House, 1951.

Frisch, Max. *Andorra.* New York: Hill & Wang, 1964.

Garton Ash, Timothy. "The Life of Death." *New York Review of Books,* December 19, 1985.

Griffin, John Howard. *Black Like Me.* Boston: Houghton Mifflin, 1961.

Griffin, Susan. *A Chorus of Stones: The Private Life of War.* New York: Doubleday, 1992.

Hilberg, Raul. *The Destruction of the European Jews*. New York: Holmes & Meier, 1985.

Hobson, Laura Z. *Gentlemen's Agreement*. New York: Simon & Schuster, 1947.

Isaac, Jules. *The Teaching of Contempt: Christian Roots of Anti-Semitism*. New York: Holt, Rinehart & Winston, 1964.

Karr, Mary. *The Art of Memoir*. New York: Harper Perennial, 2016.

Langer, Suzanne K. *Philosophy in a New Key: A Study in the Symbolism of Reason, Rite, and Art*. 3rd ed. Cambridge: Harvard University Press, 1963.

Lentin, Ronit, ed. *Gender and Catastrophe*. London: Zed Books, 1997.

Levi, Primo. *The Drowned and the Saved*, trans. Raymond Rosenthal. London: Michael Joseph, 1988.

Malamud, Bernard. *The Fixer*. New York: Farrar, Straus & Giroux, 1966.

Malcolm X, as told to Alex Haley. *The Autobiography of Malcolm X*. New York: Grove Press, 1965.

Nietzsche, Friedrich. *The Use and Abuse of History*, trans. Adrian Collins. Mineola, NY: Dover Publications, 2019.

Ofer, Dalia, and Lenore J. Weitzman, eds. *Women in the Holocaust*. New Haven: Yale University Press, 1998.

Potok, Chaim. *The Chosen*. New York: Simon & Schuster, 1967.

Redding, J. Saunders. *On Being Negro in America*. Indianapolis: Bobbs-Merrill, 1951.

Rieff, David. *Slaughterhouse: Bosnia and the Failure of the West*. New York: Simon & Schuster, 1995.

Rosenberg, Blanca. *To Tell at Last: Survival Under False Identity, 1941– 1945*. Champaign: University of Illinois Press, 1993.

Sacks, Oliver. "The Neurologist's Notebook: Prodigies." *New Yorker*, January 9, 1995.

Schama, Simon. "Clio at the Multiplex." *New Yorker*, January 19, 1998.

Schoenfeld, Gabriel. "The 'Cutting Edge' of Holocaust Studies." *Wall Street Journal*, May 21, 1998.

_____. "Auschwitz and the Professors." *Commentary*, June 1998.

Silberman, Charles E. *Crisis in Black and White*. New York: Random House, 1964.

Sontag, Susan. *Against Interpretation and Other Essays*. New York: Farrar, Straus & Giroux, 1966.

Tolstoy, Leo. *The Death of Ivan Ilyich & Other Stories*, trans. Richard Pevear and Larissa Volokhonsky. New York: Vintage Classics, 2010.

Wiesel, Elie. *Night*, trans. Stella Rodway. New York: Hill & Wang, 1960.

White, William Lindsay. *Lost Boundaries*. New York: Harcourt, Brace, 1948.

Woolf, Virginia. *A Writer's Diary*. Boston: Mariner Books, 2003.

Wright, Richard. *Native Son*. New York: Harper & Brothers, 1940.

Bibliography of Works
by Joan Ringelheim

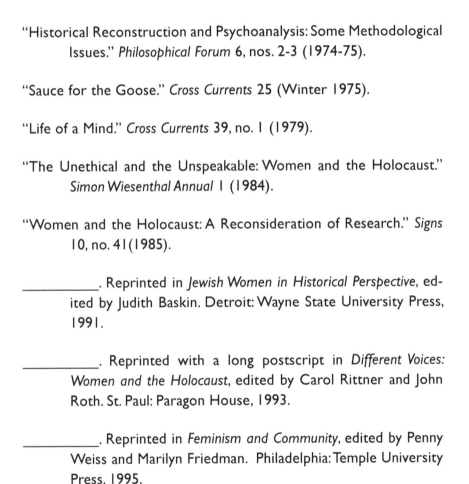

"Historical Reconstruction and Psychoanalysis: Some Methodological Issues." *Philosophical Forum* 6, nos. 2-3 (1974-75).

"Sauce for the Goose." *Cross Currents* 25 (Winter 1975).

"Life of a Mind." *Cross Currents* 39, no. 1 (1979).

"The Unethical and the Unspeakable: Women and the Holocaust." *Simon Wiesenthal Annual* 1 (1984).

"Women and the Holocaust: A Reconsideration of Research." *Signs* 10, no. 41(1985).

_____. Reprinted in *Jewish Women in Historical Perspective*, edited by Judith Baskin. Detroit: Wayne State University Press, 1991.

_____. Reprinted with a long postscript in *Different Voices: Women and the Holocaust*, edited by Carol Rittner and John Roth. St. Paul: Paragon House, 1993.

_____. Reprinted in *Feminism and Community*, edited by Penny Weiss and Marilyn Friedman. Philadelphia: Temple University Press, 1995.

"Thoughts about Women and the Holocaust." In *Thinking the*

Unthinkable: Meanings of the Holocaust, edited by Roger S. Gottlieb. Mahwah, NJ: Paulist Press, 1990.

A Catalogue of Audio and Video Collections of Holocaust Testimony, edited by Joan Ringelheim and Esther Katz. Occasional Paper of the Institute for Research in History. 2nd ed. Westport, CT: Greenwood Press, 1992.

"Deportations, Deaths and Survival: Nazi Ghetto Policies Against Jewish Women and Jewish Men in Occupied Poland." In *Nach Osten: Verdeckte Spuren nationalsozialistischer Verbrechen*, edited by Theresa Wobbe. Frankfurt am Main: Neue Kritik, 1992.

"The Holocaust: Taking Women into Account." *Jewish Quarterly* (Autumn 1992).

"Genocide and Gender: A Split Memory." In *Gender and Catastrophe*, edited by Ronit Lentin. London: Zed Books, 1997.

"Kratko Putovanje u Sarajevo u Sienci Holokausta." In *Um*, edited by Haris Pašović. Sarajevo: Mess and Saint, 1997.

"The Split Between Gender and Genocide." In *Women in the Holocaust*, edited by Dalia Ofer and Lenore J. Weitzman. New Haven: Yale University Press, 1998.

"The Strange and the Familiar." In *Humanity at the Limit: The Impact of the Holocaust Experience on Jews and Christians*, edited by Michael A. Signer. Bloomington: Indiana University Press, 2000.

"The Holocaust in My Life." In *Her Story, My Story? Writing about Women and the Holocaust*, edited by Judith Tydor Baumel-Schwartz and Dalia Ofer. Bern and New York: Peter Lang, 2020.

Acknowledgements

A number of people important to me read parts of the manuscript, raised important questions, offered critical comments or helped with the accuracy of my memory. Their responses were more than helpful. I thank Sally Hanley, Neenah Ellis, Alexandra Zapruder, Edna McCown, Nancy McKenzie, Charlie Munitz, Gayle Young, Suada Kapic, Sarah Ogilvie, Keren Blankfeld, Betty Bullock, Ted Ringelheim, Ellen Carr, Lucy Kerewsky and Stan Wenocur.

The person I most want to thank is Joy Johannessen, my editor. Joy was in two of my classes at DePauw University when I taught there in 1968 and was known as unusually gifted to faculty, even as a second-year student. After I left DePauw, she became a good and close friend. Joy was editor at Chelsea House, Grove Press; and the executive editor of Delphinium Books. She edited such authors as Harold Bloom, Michael Cunningham, Larry Kramer, Ursula K. Le Guin, Arthur Miller, Ralph Nader and Hector Tobar. She now freelances. When I knew that these essays would be completed, I could not imagine a better person to edit my work. I was thrilled that she agreed to do it. Joy's understanding of my history, her enormous intelligence and sensitivity, her ability to find the strengths and problems in a text, her comments, queries and revisions made it possible for these essays to be a genuine reflection of my experiences and thoughts as they are at this moment.

CPSIA information can be obtained
at www.ICGtesting.com
Printed in the USA
BVHW071340221121
622225BV00002B/73